Faith
Over
Fear

JOURNAL AND BOOK

Faith Over Fear: Youth edition
Journal and Book

Published in 2022 by Dawnlight Publishing

ISBN 978-1-99-117707-0 (paperback)
ISBN 978-1-99-117690-5 (hardcover)

Text © Kataleya Graceal 2022
Book design © Dream Co Media 2022
The moral right of the author has been asserted.
Sketch artwork doves by Mary Marinan

Faith Over Fear

JOURNAL AND BOOK

FIND HOPE IN THE MIDDLE

OF DIFFICULT TIMES

Kataleya Graceal

DAWNLIGHT
PUBLISHING

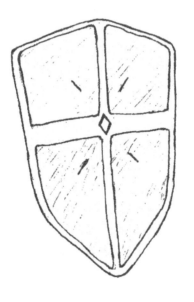

DEDICATION AND THANK YOU

This book is dedicated to Jesus, who is Hope,
a shining Light and loving Saviour.

Thank you to all my dear readers, friends
and family for your love and support in
bringing this 'message of hope' book to life.
I appreciate all of you, and your love and
prayers. God bless.

Contents

Introduction

1 **In The Midst**

2 **Faith Over Fear**

3 Protection

4 Rest

5 Light in the Darkness

6 Safety

7 Trust

8 Strength

9 Hope

10 **Healing**

11 God's Goodness

12 Peace

13 **Help**

14 **Worship**

15 The Day Will Come

Prayer

Connection

God is our refuge and
strength, a very present
help in trouble.

Psalm 46:1 KJV

THIS BOOK AND JOURNAL BELONGS TO:

Name:

_____

Date: _____

Bible translation currently reading in:

_____

Favourite Bible verse:

_____

Church or home group name:

_____

Country living in:

_____

Dear Reader

Hello! Did you know that you are awesome? Well, God certainly thinks so, and so do I!

Welcome to this youth edition of *Faith Over Fear*, a brand-new book just for you! I pray that you find hope and faith in God as you read these encouraging Bible verses and my story.

This is an updated version of a book I wrote when the pandemic first happened called: *Faith Over Fear: Finding Hope in the Midst of a Pandemic*. It quickly became an Amazon number one bestseller, with readers finding it a great source of encouragement with specific verses to reflect on. It was written with an urgency in my heart that people needed words of hope, faith and truth found in God's Word to hold onto during this time.

The Bible is where we can find God's light in the

midst of turbulent times, and to be encouraged to hold on strongly to the truth and assurances of His promises for His people.

Faith comes from hearing, and hearing

through the word of Christ.

Romans 10: 17 ESV

This book is scripture-filled, alongside my testimony, with encouraging chapter titles like Protection, Safety, Hope, Faith Over Fear, Peace and more.

Excitedly, this edition is now also a journal with space where you can engage with the subject in each chapter by answering reflection questions, and writing your own prayers and thoughts.

It gives you opportunity to reflect on each chapter title through writing, and the accompanying Bible verses, and spend time with God soaking in His love and truths to hold onto during these times. Journaling what you are going through with God becomes a special, personal experience.

Look out for this feather pen icon to indicate the journaling sections.

In these next chapters, you'll find encouraging verses from the Bible in different translations about God's love, hope and protection.

The Bible is where we can find truth and anchor our hope in Jesus as we read God's promises found in the Word of God.

The Lord recently showed me that peace and comfort found in God's Word during stormy times is like someone coming in from a cold snow blizzard, into a house filled with warmth and a lit fireplace.

Can you imagine the feeling – from feeling frozen, alone, barely able to see what's happening through the snowstorm, and not at all comfortable...to then stepping into warmth, shelter and comfort, resting by a warm fireplace.

I pray that you feel renewed in God's unconditional love and grace as you read this book and find hope for all the good things He's got in store for you, no matter what the current situation looks like.

God is understanding of what you're going through during this pandemic.

God cares for you, so turn all

your worries over to him.

1 Peter 5:7 CEV

So like David, who wasn't afraid to face Goliath and trusted more in the power of his God instead of cowering in the face of a strong giant, let's stand together united in hope and faith. And let's not be afraid, but instead trust that God is going to bring us through redemptively, powerfully, healed, whole and looking forward to a bright new future ahead.

Dearest reader – my heart is with yours as you read this book. Let's take the journey together to choose faith in God over fear each day!

See you in the next pages!

' Through our darkest night can **shine the brightest light**. **Hope** has a name. That name is **Jesus**.'

In the Midst

'Yet in the midst of great darkness there

is tremendous **hope** in God...'

At the time of writing this, it is now 2022. In 2020 a world-wide pandemic had been declared, with many countries going into lockdown, as a new virus swept the globe infecting and killing many people. At present, our country is no longer in full lockdown, but there are still people isolating, restrictions and mask-wearing. And, there are other countries that are still in lockdown, and different variants of the virus have emerged, causing the pandemic to still be on-going at this present time.

On top of the pandemic, there are now other major events occurring in the nations causing further unrest.

Normal day-to-day life seems like a distant

memory now, and many might still be wondering what happens next in the future. It seems like normal as we knew it may not return the same way – but rest assured, God is still the same! God's love for us hasn't run out, nor His good plans for our lives, and His loving arms are open towards you.

I pray that in this time of darkness – instead of being caught up in fear – you'll find your faith greatly strengthened, soak deeply in the grace of God, find hope in His Word, and rest in God's welcoming arms, staying close to His heart. God's heart is for you, and He longs to draw you close to Him during this time.

Cast your burden on the LORD,

And He shall sustain you;

He shall never permit the righteous

to be moved.

Psalm 55: 22 NKJV

Welcome to the start of your journaling journey, looking at the topic of faith and hope in the Lord versus fear. To start with, note the date, your current situation, or what you are currently going through:

_____

_____

_____

_____

_____

_____

_____

_____

_____

_____

_____

_____

_____

_____

_____

_____

_____

_____

_____

_____

Faith Over Fear

How are you feeling at the moment?

_____

_____

_____

_____

_____

_____

Remembering how God has helped you before can help to build faith for the future, to know God will come through for you again.

Note how God has helped you so far during this pandemic, how He is helping you through your current situation, or a faith statement about trusting in God that He's going to bring breakthrough for whatever you need in the future:

_____

_____

_____

_____

_____

_____

_____

_____

_____

Faith Over Fear

Journal any other thoughts, prayers and verses about being **in the midst** of a pandemic:

_____

_____

_____

_____

_____

_____

_____

_____

_____

_____

_____

_____

_____

_____

_____

_____

_____

_____

_____

_____

_____

"Be **strong** and of good **courage**,
do not fear nor be afraid of them;
for the **Lord your God**, He *is*
the One who goes with you. He
will not leave you nor forsake you."

Deuteronomy 31:6 NKJV

Faith Over Fear

When we're faced with a situation that is scary, it is natural to feel fear at first. For example, if we came across a large, wild animal, a natural fear instinctively kicks in to give you wisdom to stay at a distance rather than go up and say hello.

There is also a natural reverential fear we have of the Lord – one that's not in fear of punishment, but in awe and in respect of who God is in all His might.

But when fear that's not from the Lord starts to consume people's minds, it becomes tormenting. The devil uses fear to latch on with sharp talons – to try and keep people afraid, unable to move forward, caged-in in their thoughts and not living in faith, trust, and hope in God.

The same thing happened when the pandemic

first arrived and everyone around the world started to hear about this virus – fear exploded and became an issue too. Anxiety rose exponentially due to this external stress-filled situation.

I deeply understand what you are feeling, if you too have been through or are presently going through a time when you feel great fear and anxiety, as I have personally experienced a season where it felt like I was under spiritual attack with constant panic attacks that were trying to derail my destiny and purpose in God. But I also know the mighty power of God to break us free from the traps of fear, and to bring us through by His saving light; into His love, grace, freedom, hope and truth!

We overcome by the blood of the Lamb and the word of our testimony (Revelation 12:11).

For we are not fighting against flesh-and-blood enemies, but against evil rulers and authorities of the unseen world, against mighty powers in this dark world, and against evil spirits in the

heavenly places.

Ephesians 6: 12 NLT

Can I share something interesting about what fear looks like... One year there was an annual women's church conference coming up, but I was so inundated with panic attacks, feeling gripped both mentally and physically, that I literally wasn't able to go.

It was one of many intense attacks that came after starting a writing journey to inspire and help people. The strange thing was, was that these experiences made me feel like I wasn't myself. It didn't feel natural. I'm usually calm, so to feel anxious, not able to breathe well, often dizzy, and unable to do life how I usually would wasn't normal. Like I was being suffocated by many traumatic events that also followed.

When this would happen, I'd usually find a way to push through in prayer and determination, and not let the enemy stop me attending something important, but this time couldn't make it.

That's when the Lord showed me a vision of a very large snake wrapped around me in the spiritual realm! Not cool, right!

I'm not a fan of scary-looking snakes, but seeing this wasn't scary then – it was revelatory. That what I was experiencing wasn't just me that was running away with my thoughts, but in fact there was a demonic attack that was trying to stop me. To keep me away from having a wonderful time with my friends, worshipping together, getting dressed up, and having fun and being refreshed as often happens at ladies conferences.

I didn't win the battle that day to go out, but God took me on a journey of learning truth, deeper levels of His grace, tools to conquer anxiety and how to live in freedom, growing in Him, and seeing fear for what it is – a boa constrictor, and that terrorizing fear is not from God.

In 2 Timothy 1:7, the Word is clear and encouraging where it says, *'God hath not given us a spirit of fear; but of power, and of love, and of a sound mind.'* (KJV)

love

power

sound mind

Another encouraging verse from Isaiah 54: 17 in the NKJV is:

"No weapon formed against you

shall prosper"

A very powerful tool is reading and speaking out God's truth found in the Bible.

The Word of God, that contains powerful and lifesaving scriptures to anchor our hope in, is described as *alive and active, sharper than any double-edge sword* (Hebrews 4:12 NIV).

It's so important during a crisis to hold onto God's Word. The Bible is trustworthy just like it's author, God, our Creator.

The featured scripture in Deuteronomy, at the start of this chapter, gives us such great encouragement to be strong and of good courage.

This verse was written about Moses speaking to all of Israel. They were yet to cross over to the promised land, and Moses told them that God was going to cross over before them, and to be courageous when they went and not to be afraid of the people there.

God doesn't want us to be afraid because He is the One who's with us.

The NKJV translation, in the next featured scripture, puts emphasis on this by mentioning a few times that it is God who goes with you, starting with, 'For the Lord your God' and following with 'He is the One'. Then it says, 'He will be with you.'

"Be **strong** and of **good courage**, do not
fear nor be afraid of them; for **the
Lord your God**, He *is* the One who
goes with you. He will not leave you
nor forsake you."
Then Moses called Joshua and said to
him in the sight of all Israel, "**Be strong
and of good courage**, for you must go
with this people to the land which the
Lord has sworn to their fathers to **give**
them, and you shall cause them to inherit
it. And the Lord, **He *is* the One who
goes before you**. He will be with you,
He will not leave you nor forsake you;
do not fear nor be dismayed."
Deuteronomy 31: 6-8

As the situation around the world still keeps
changing on a daily basis, it can be easy to or
seem normal to get caught up in anxiety,
depression and worry as we watch what's still
happening at a global pace. And now more than
ever, it's so important to hold onto what God says
in His Word, the Bible.

Together, let's choose FAITH over FEAR.

For we walk by **faith**, not by sight.

2 Corinthians 5: 7 KJV

Having faith in God during these times is trusting Him to work it all out. To let go of uncertainty and let God be our rock in every circumstance.

Faith in action can be like playing a board game in life. We have paths to choose from, and 'game pieces' to put forward. When obstacles come along, we can choose what to respond with in each circumstantial turn; hope, trust, grace, love, faith.

In this pandemic you might be faced with what to choose to lift up in the face of fear that's come about circumstantially. I'll tell you which one currently stands out for me the most in light of current events, later on in the book.

Now **faith** is the substance of things **hoped for**, the evidence of things not seen. For by it the elders obtained a good report. Through **faith** we understand that the worlds were framed by the word of God, so that

things which are seen were not made
of things which do appear.
Hebrews 11: 1-3 KJV

*I pray that because of the riches of His shining-
greatness, He will make you strong with power in your
hearts through the Holy Spirit.* **I pray that Christ may
live in your hearts by faith.** *I pray that you will be
filled with love. I pray that you will be able to
understand how wide and how long and how high and
how deep His love is. I pray that you will know the
love of Christ. His love goes beyond anything we can
understand. I pray that you will be filled with*

God Himself.

**God is able to do much more than we ask or think
through His power working in us.** *May we see His
shining-greatness in the church. May all people in all
time honor Christ Jesus. Let it be so.*

Ephesians 3: 16 – 21 NLV

Let's look at Deuteronomy 31:8 in a variety of translations to capture an in depth look at this verse.

Write out this verse in your favourite Bible translation:

_____

_____

_____

_____

_____

Choose two other translations you like and write out these verses:

_____

_____

_____

_____

_____

_____

_____

_____

_____

_____

_____

_____

Circle the words in these verses that stand out to you the most. Write the circled words here:

_____

_____

_____

_____

_____

_____

_____

Hold onto these words dearly like treasure that brings life and comfort in God.

God Can Remove the 'Un' From Any Situation

Common words that have been floating around since it all began are ones like 'uncertainty', 'unknown' and 'uncharted', with the stand-out in communications being that 'this is an unprecedented situation'. Many will be feeling like their lives have become undone. For those who have lost their jobs and their feeling of stability, and especially those who have lost loved ones – you'll be going through unbearable pain.

But please know God is right there with you. He is greater than the darkness, He is more than able to save and help, and loves you *dearly*. You can look to Him for hope and to take away the 'un' from those words:

Uncertainty to certainty – certainty in God.

Unbearable to bearable – this situation is bearable in God's loving arms as He walks you through this difficult time.

Unknown to known – lovingly known by God, and especially; knowing who God is, and that He is in control and wants to set people free from fear of the unknown. You can trust Him.

Certainty

Being certain of a good future comes through hoping in God. We can't make it happen by our own efforts. Rest in what Jesus has already done for you on the cross, and that He is mighty and able to save. Let Him fill your heart with courage and trust in Him.

I'm sure the writer of these next verses in

Lamentations can relate and identify with being in pain and yet having hope in God:

I will never forget this awful time,

as I grieve over my loss.

Yet I still dare to hope

when I remember this:

The faithful love of the Lord never ends!

His mercies never cease.

Great is his faithfulness;

his mercies begin afresh each morning.

Lamentations 3: 20-23 NLT

Bearable

I felt quite emotional writing this paragraph and in tears as my heart breaks for those that have lost loved ones in this pandemic. Especially for those in countries that have funeral attendance restrictions and therefore can't attend their loved ones' funeral or be near family and friends for comfort. It must be a heart-wrenching time in the midst of chaos.

But how much more does God want to draw close to you, knowing the pain you're going through in these dark times? Jesus himself suffered greatly and knew what great pain and sorrow felt like as He died for us on that cross.

Reach out to Him who is your ever-present help in your time of need. Let Him comfort you with words of love, hope and encouragement.

Known

You are known by God, loved dearly by Him, and by releasing the fear of the unknown – you can instead trust in God that He knows the future and that He has great plans instore for you. God won't leave you in despair, but gives you hope for the future.

For I know the thoughts that I think

toward you, says the Lord,

thoughts of **peace** and not of evil,

to give you a future and a hope.

Jeremiah 29:11 NKJV

Stay encouraged – there are good days ahead.

Another translation says, 'For I know the plans I have for you':

"For I know the plans I have for you,"

declares the Lord,

"plans to prosper you and not to harm

you, **plans to give you hope** and a future."

Jeremiah 29:11 NIV

In Proverbs 23 it says there is a future hope:

There is surely a future hope for

you, and your hope will not

be cut off.

Proverbs 23:18 NIV

I called upon the Lord in distress: the Lord

answered me, and set me in a large place.

The Lord is on my side; I will not fear: what

can man do unto me?

Psalm 118: 5-6a KJV

Can you identify with any of the words mentioned above like 'uncertainty', fear of the 'unknown', or any others that have tried to bring stress into your life like feeling 'unsettled' or 'unimportant'?

Write them out here without the 'un' and draw a circle around each one. This signifies God's tremendous love for you. You are seen, not alone and you are important to God – incredibly so.

Choosing FAITH over FEAR

Choosing faith over fear feels like a call to stand strong in faith during these times, and not to buckle in fear.

A call to allow God to strengthen our faith in Him like no other, and to shine with His light in the darkness to others.

A call to rest in faith in God as our Saviour (and ultimate world problem-solver). Therefore, we don't have to take it all upon ourselves to try and fix anything, or be constantly in fear. Instead, knowing by the power of *His* grace, that our faith isn't in ourselves to solve this global problem but instead it's in Him.

In 1 John 4: 16-18 it talks about there being no fear in love, that perfect love casts out fear.

If God loves us and God is love, and we are in Him, then there's nothing to fear.

You don't need to fear a bad news report, a situation that looks scary, or anything that might try and shake you from your faith in God, because the tremendous love of God will sustain you.

Let's look at a wonderful verse about who God is, and that there is no fear in love!

We know and have believed the love which God has for us. God is love, and he who remains in love remains in God, and God remains in him. In this, love has been made perfect among us, that we may have boldness in the day of judgment, because as he is, even so we are in this world. There is no fear in love; *but perfect love casts out fear, because fear has punishment. He who fears is not made perfect in love.*

1 John 4: 16 – 18 WEB

As we study the topic of faith in this chapter and book, you might be wondering if you need to muster up a lot of faith to get through any tough days.

But in the next verse, Jesus assures us that with just a small amount of faith like a mustard seed, we can move a mountain. It also talks about the power of our words.

For truly, I say to you, if you have faith

like a grain of mustard seed, you will

say to this mountain, 'Move from here

to there,' and it will move, and

nothing will be impossible for you.

Matthew 17: 20b ESV

Isn't this incredible! He can take the little faith we choose to have in Him and turn it into something wonderous, something powerful! Imagine what God can do with a lot of faith.

But this is something that we don't need to be burdened by – to try and make ourselves have great faith out of our own striving efforts. Instead, God is the founder, the one who initiates and perfects our faith, and faith comes by hearing the Word of God.

Faith cometh by hearing, and

hearing by the word of God.

Romans 10: 17 KJV

It's something by grace, that God can do within us – in our relationship with Him – as we yield and trust Him to grow our faith, as we begin to see mountain after mountain move!

For it is by free grace (God's unmerited favor) that you are saved delivered from judgment *and* made partakers of Christ's salvation) through [your] faith. And this [salvation] is not of yourselves [of your own doing, it came not through your own striving], but it is the gift of God

Ephesians 2: 8-9 AMPC

*Let us run with endurance the race that is set before us, **looking to Jesus**, the founder and perfecter of our faith, who for the joy that was set before him endured the cross, despising the shame, and is seated at the right hand of the throne of God.*

Hebrews 12: 1b – 2 ESV

Before this crisis happened, I'd been drawn to see lots of verses about protection in the Bible. About being sheltered under God's wings. Usually I would wake up with a Psalm in mind to go to on a particular day, and at the time I thought God was talking about a particular stressful situation that was happening before the pandemic hit.

Those verses were encouraging for that situation also, but I now see He was alluding to things to come.

In the book of Psalms there are many verses that encourage us to not be afraid and I'd love to share this one. If the Lord is on our side, then we can choose to have faith over fear!

> "Fear not, for I have redeemed you;
> I have called *you* by your name;
> You *are* Mine.
> When you pass through the waters,
> I *will be* with you;
> And through the rivers,
> they shall not overflow you.
> When you walk through the fire,
> you shall not be burned,
> Nor shall the flame scorch you.
> For I *am* the LORD your God,
> The Holy One of Israel, your Savior.
>
> Fear not, for I am with you."
> Isaiah 43: 1b -3a & 5 NKJV

What does living in faith instead of fear look and/or feel like to you? Write this out or draw a picture about what it looks or feels like:

_____

_____

_____

_____

_____

_____

_____

Journal any other thoughts, prayers and verses about having **faith over fear** in a pandemic:

_____

_____

_____

_____

_____

_____

_____

_____

_____

_____

_____

_____

_____

_____

_____

_____

_____

_____

_____

_____

FAITH OVER FEAR

Protection

In Psalm 91 it says to not be afraid even though many may fall. In the context where worldwide many thousands upon thousands of people have suddenly died, this verse now seems extremely real.

But have hope!

There are many verses in the Bible that talks about God's protection. In fact, the whole of Psalm ninety-one is specifically devoted to this topic and being under the sheltering wings of God's protection. Let's see what it says about being safe in Him...

He that dwelleth in the secret place of the
most High shall abide under the shadow of
the Almighty.

*I will say of the Lord, He is my refuge and
my fortress: my God; in him will I trust.*
Surely he shall deliver thee from the snare of
the fowler, and from the noisome pestilence.
He shall cover thee with his feathers, and
under his wings shalt thou trust: his truth
shall be thy shield and buckler.
Thou shalt not be afraid for the terror by
night; nor for the arrow that flieth by day;
Nor for the pestilence that walketh in
darkness; nor for the destruction that
wasteth at noonday.
A thousand shall fall at thy side, and
ten thousand at thy right hand; but it shall
not come nigh thee.
Only with thine eyes shalt thou behold and
see the reward of the wicked.

Because thou hast made the Lord, which is
my refuge, even the most High, thy habitation;
There shall no evil befall thee, neither shall
any plague come nigh thy dwelling.
For he shall give his angels charge over thee,
to keep thee in all thy ways.
They shall bear thee up in their hands,
lest thou dash thy foot against a stone.
Thou shalt tread upon the lion and adder:
the young lion and the dragon shalt thou
trample under feet.
Because he hath set his love upon me,
therefore will I deliver him: I will set him
on high, because he hath known my name.
He shall call upon me, and I will answer him:
I will be with him in trouble; I will deliver him,
and honour him.
With long life will I satisfy him, and
shew him my salvation.
Psalm 91 KJV

In another translation of Psalm 91, the NLV, it says about God being a safe and strong place, and that God is faithful like a strong wall.

He who lives in the safe place of the

Most High will be in the shadow of

the All-powerful. I will say to the Lord,

"**You are my safe and strong place**,

my God, in Whom I trust." For it

is He Who takes you away from the

trap, and from the killing sickness.

He will cover you with His wings.

And **under His wings you will be safe**.

He is faithful like a safe-covering and

a strong wall.

Psalm 91: 1-4 NLV

In verse 11 of Psalm 91, God gives us an amazing assurance that His angels are protecting us.

What stands out for me in this verse in the NKJV is 'all of your ways', and in the CEV translation it says 'wherever you go'. So God doesn't promise to protect us just sometimes or only in some places, but in ALL of our ways, wherever we go. Amazing!

For He shall give His angels

charge over you,

To keep you in all your ways.

In *their* hands they shall bear you up

Psalm 91 11-12a NKJV

God will command his angels

to **protect** you

wherever you go.

They will carry you

in their arms

Psalm 91:11-12a (CEV)

Our inner selves wait [earnestly] for the

Lord; He is our Help and our Shield.

For in Him does our heart rejoice,

because we have trusted (relied on and

been confident) in His holy name.

Psalm 33: 20-21 AMPC

A number of times in my life, I've experienced God's protection in a miraculous way.

I remember once when I was driving home in my car, and I was travelling towards a connecting highway. Just before the on-ramp I had to go past an intersection where other cars wanting to join the road had to giveway and then merge with the lane I was driving in to then join the highway.

But as I neared this intersection, suddenly another car pulled out in front of me!

Instead of waiting for me to pass and join the lane when there was a gap, they'd drastically and dangerously pulled out too soon. And the problem was I was going the speed limit but much faster than they were, and they were going way too slow as their car attempted to join the lane of traffic.

I'd slammed on my brakes, but knew in that moment there was no way I wouldn't collide with the other car who was only travelling at about a quarter of my car's speed. But by some miracle – and to this day I still don't know how – my car managed to suddenly slow down and not crash into the car in front!

I didn't see any angels, but I knew they were there. It all happened so fast, but just as quick I knew that in the natural I should have crashed, but supernaturally God had stopped my car as if time and space had changed! God is outside time and can save in such amazing ways!

I was a new Christian at the time, and still learning a lot, but to me it was simply undeniable, with God showing me early on in my relationship with Him that He supernaturally protects us. And while I was amazed, it also felt normal in a sense that this is what God does.

Since then, I've experienced other similar situations where miracles of protection have happened by just a whisper of measurement, and God's miraculous healing time and time again, and continue to praise God for His incredible protection.

I think it's a great reminder to remember all the amazing things God has done and is doing for us in our lives. As it builds our faith during times of distress, to remember that if God has done it before then He'll surely come through for us again. His protection over us isn't limited, but always everlasting. Let's praise God and thank Him for His loving protection over us at all times.

For He will tell His angels to care for
you and keep you in all your ways.

They will hold you up in their hands.

So your foot will not hit against a stone.

You will walk upon the lion and the snake.

You will crush under your feet the young lion

and the snake.

Psalm 91: 11-13 NLV

Here are some more wonderful verses from the Psalms that assure us of God's refuge and being defended by Him.

Blessed are all who take refuge in him.

Psalm 2: 12d ESV

Let all those rejoice who put their
trust in You;
Let them ever shout for joy,
because You defend them;
Let those also who love Your
name be joyful in You.
For You, O Lord, will bless the
righteous; With favor You will
surround him as *with* a shield.
Psalm 5: 11 – 12 NKJV

PROTECTION

Wow! Theses scriptures have really fuelled me with hope and peace, and I hope they have encouraged you also – that we can trust in God's powerful protection during this pandemic, being under His sheltering wings.

Here's another amazing Psalm that talks about God as our Protector:

I love you, Lord; you are my strength.

The Lord is my rock, my fortress, and

my savior; my God is my rock,

in whom I find protection.

He is my shield, the power that

saves me, and my place of safety.

I called on the Lord, who is worthy

of praise, and he saved me from

my enemies.

Psalm 18: 1-3 NLT

The angel of the Lord encamps all around

those who fear Him, And delivers them.

Psalm 34:7 NKJV

Recently I've been thinking about an amazing event in the Bible. It's the one in 2 Kings 6: 14-17 about Elisha and his servant who were surrounded by a great army trying to seize Elisha. Elisha's servant freaked out, asking what they should do.

But Elisha responded with something incredible, saying, 'Do not be afraid, for those who are with us are more than those who are with them.' He then prayed and asked God to open his servant's eyes, and when God opened them he saw that the mountain was full of horses and chariots of fire all around Elisha!

As I study this more, what stands out is that firstly Elisha said don't be afraid. So, don't worry about is happening in the natural, and what that might look like, because what is happening in the supernatural realm is incredible! While we can't see supernaturally all the time, God's guardian angels are there. And God doesn't want us to be afraid.

It is comforting to know that we are protected as those that dwell under the sheltering of the wings of the Most High. In the presence of the Holy Spirit who is with us, always; we are protected, safe and there's no better place to be!

PROTECTION

Write out the whole of Psalm 91 in your favourite
Bible translation. Then highlight what verses stand
out to you the most:

_____

_____

_____

_____

_____

_____

_____

_____

_____

_____

_____

_____

_____

_____

_____

_____

_____

_____

_____

_____

_____

Faith Over Fear

_____

_____

_____

_____

_____

_____

_____

_____

_____

_____

_____

_____

_____

_____

_____

_____

_____

_____

_____

_____

_____

_____

_____

_____

PROTECTION

Write out a prayer of protection for a loved one:

_____

_____

_____

_____

_____

_____

_____

_____

_____

_____

_____

_____

_____

_____

_____

_____

_____

_____

_____

_____

Look up a song that describes God as our protector, the One who we can run to, and write out any lyrics that stand out to you:

_____

_____

_____

_____

_____

_____

_____

_____

_____

_____

_____

_____

_____

_____

_____

_____

_____

_____

_____

_____

Write out any other prayers, thoughts and reflections about God's **protection**:

_____

_____

_____

_____

_____

_____

_____

_____

_____

_____

_____

_____

_____

_____

_____

_____

_____

_____

_____

_____

_____

Rest

While many of us are now in the situation of staying at home to isolate at times, it's a great opportunity to find rest: to rest physically from the usual busyness of life, but to also rest in the Lord and wait on Him. And as you wait on the Lord, He'll renew your strength like having winds of refreshment in your wings – to soar like eagles with powerful outspread wings, high above this darkness.

> They that wait upon the LORD
>
> shall renew their strength;
>
> they shall mount up with
>
> wings as eagles; they shall run,
>
> and not be weary, and they shall
>
> walk, and not faint.
>
> Isaiah 40: 31 KJV

Isn't that incredible! Eagles are amazing birds that are high-altitude flyers, and are also perceptive – they can tell when a storm is coming, and rise up above it before it hits!

Let's be like eagles and step away from the chaos and overwhelming fear that tries to take a grip on our lives, and instead enter into God's presence, with thanksgiving, to feel *rested*, well, and at peace again.

There's another translation that says 'those who hope' in the Lord.

> Those who hope in the LORD
> will renew their strength.
> **They will soar on wings like eagles**;
> they will run and not grow weary,
> they will walk and not be faint.
>
> Isaiah 40: 31 NIV

The Bible also says it's good to wait on God. Let's be at rest in His presence, knowing He is God.

Shifting our focus towards the Lord can be where we find peace as our thoughts on the pandemic chaos fades away.

The L ORD is **good** unto them that wait
for Him, to the soul that seeketh Him.
It is good that a man should both **hope**
and quietly wait for the salvation of
the L ORD .

Lamentations 3: 25-26 KJ21

Be still, and know that I *am* God;
I will be exalted among the nations,
I will be exalted in the earth!

Psalm 46: 10 NKJV

Jesus wants us to come to Him to rest if we are
feeling overwhelmed:

Come to me, all who labor and are heavy
burdened, and **I will give you rest**. Take my yoke
upon you, and learn from me, for I am gentle and
lowly in heart, and you will find rest for your souls.
For my yoke is easy, and my burden is light.

Matthew 11: 28 – 30 WEB

Let us labour therefore

to enter into that rest.

Hebrews 4: 11 KJV

Being at home more often is an opportunity to enjoy the things you might not otherwise have time for.

It can be nice to find rest in God while spending time with Him like in the simplicity of looking out the window and seeing something new. Keeping our minds off the bad news of the current events and focusing on good things instead.

Being surrounded by nature and all of God's beautiful creation, and enjoying activities, can bring health to our bodies and minds as we unwind. Listening to birds chirping away in the garden. Sitting near the ocean and watching the waves. Seeing the moon appear as evening draws in, or stargaze on a still, cloudless night. Baking those delicious cookies! Listening to your favourite music on repeat. Noticing the beautiful colours in nature and intricacies in their design. Watching a sunrise or sunset.

This is something I'd love to do – actually watch the sun set one evening!

My family has been isolating this week, and the weather has been rainy and stormy which has made it a little easier for us to stay indoors.

Today, as I was writing this new update, a sunshower that appeared that was really pretty. I've taken the opportunity to watch the rain falling outside while sitting next to my cat, who is happy to snooze on the sofa all day. There has been lots of birds in the garden, happily hopping along, no doubt enjoying the breaks in the weather when the sun shines. It's a small thing, but I find it's been peaceful and lovely just to sit and 'be' for a moment outside of the business of life.

There remains therefore a **rest** for

the people of God.

Hebrews 4: 9 NKJV

There's something amazingly powerful about being spiritually at rest in our hearts too. When we take a posture of rest in our hearts and minds, and leave our worries in the good Lord's hands, we can deeply trust in God and His saving grace.

God loves to see His precious children at rest and not stressed. God wants us at rest in Him.

Faith Over Fear

God's people have a complete rest waiting for

them. The man who goes into God's rest,

rests from his own work the same as

God rested from His work.

Let us do our best to go into that rest or

we will be like the people who did not go in.

Hebrews 4: 9-11 NLV

The Lord is my shepherd;

I have all that I need.

He lets me rest in green meadows;

he leads me beside peaceful streams.

He renews my strength.

He guides me along right paths,

bringing honor to his name.

Psalm 23: 1-3 NLT

He who dwells in the secret place of

the Most High will rest in the shadow

of the Almighty.

Psalm 91:1 WEB

REST

Praise God for all these awesome scriptures about resting in Him. Write down what true rest in the Lord looks like to you?

_____

_____

_____

_____

_____

_____

_____

_____

_____

_____

_____

_____

_____

_____

_____

_____

_____

_____

_____

_____

_____

_____

Very early on in the Bible, in Genesis 2: 2-3, God talks about rest. He Himself rested on the seventh day because all of creation was complete, and He blessed and declared this day Holy. Imagine what that day of rest might have been like for God and creation, and write down any thoughts:

_____

_____

_____

_____

_____

_____

_____

_____

_____

_____

_____

_____

_____

_____

_____

_____

_____

_____

REST

Pen your thoughts, prayers and verses about **resting** in God:

_____

_____

_____

_____

_____

_____

_____

_____

_____

_____

_____

_____

_____

_____

_____

_____

_____

_____

_____

_____

_____

_____

REST

Light in the Darkness

Jesus spoke to all the people, saying,

"I am the Light of the world. Anyone who

follows Me will not walk in darkness.

He will have the **Light of Life**."

John 8: 12 NLV

Jesus said to them, "The light is

among you for a little while longer.

Walk while you have the light,

lest darkness overtake you. The one

who walks in the darkness does not

know where he is going."

John 12: 35 ESV

In Micah 7:8, the author and prophet, Micah, describes feeling down because of his enemies but he had a powerful response:

> Do not have joy over me, you who
>
> hate me. When I fall, I will rise.
>
> Even though I am in darkness,
>
> **the Lord will be my light.** (NLV)

As great darkness is still spreading across the whole world, it can sometimes seem as though the darkness could take over. That you too might be swept up in the worst-case scenario of what's happening, with businesses suddenly closing and many dying, or be overwhelmed by fear of how the future might look.

But what's the first thing we do when we're in a dark room? We turn on a light. We need light in dark times to see where to go, and God's light gives us this direction.

Recently, I was travelling somewhere at night, but my destination was in a rural location where there weren't many streetlights along the sides of the road.

The further I drove, the darker it seemed to get at

night, and it was hard to see the signs indicating the names of the roads I was passing.

I wanted to slow down each time I came across a new sign to see if it was the right road I needed to turn into, without passing it by, which wasn't easy to do with the main road being a high-speed area and cars travelling behind me. So I couldn't slow down too much if it wasn't the right road to turn off into.

I was going somewhere new, and I even thought to give up trying to find the place as I wasn't familiar with the area, it was hard to see at night time, and I didn't know if I'd missed the right road to turn into. It was only supposed to be a short drive according to the map I'd looked at beforehand, but it seemed like I'd been driving for a long time.

Eventually, I saw the church where I was going to lit up ahead. It was a shining beacon in the midst of the night-time darkness, and not only was it helping me to see where it was in the distance, there was enough light coming from the building that I could also see the right road to turn into.

This got me thinking about how we are the light in the darkness, and if all of God's people as a global church are shining brightly together in unity, how big will the beacon of light and hope be in the midst of this pandemic!

Many are becoming wary due to the longevity of it, and yet as we've found this hope in Jesus, it's so important to share this with those that aren't yet saved.

This *hope* we have as an anchor of the

soul, both sure and steadfast

Hebrews 6: 19 NKJV

Like the first verse in this chapter that says Jesus is the light of the world, we can share about Jesus being a guiding light people can look to in the midst of darkness.

In John 14: 6 it says Jesus is the way: *Jesus said to him, "I am the way, and the truth, and the life." (ESV).* You can look to Jesus to see where to go in an everchanging environment, and encourage others to do so too.

In God's Word there are amazing scriptures about light and His Word – the Bible itself is a light and a lamp:

Your word is a lamp to my feet,

and a **light** for my path.

Psalm 119: 105 WEB

Your Word is a lamp to my feet. How wonderful is this – that God's Word offers light and direction. If you feel like you don't know where to go next – look to God's Word for direction.

It might look like doom and gloom from one perspective, but rest assured God has a different view.

He's already in the future and knows the right direction for His precious children to go in, and already has good solutions ready and prepared for you. His Word is watering – lifegiving. It brings refreshment and revelation, like much-needed water in a desert and illumination at night. So jump on into the river of living water and let God refresh you to be His light in the darkness.

The Word says Jesus is the Light that has come into this world and the One who came to save the world.

In these next verses, Jesus mentions faith in Him and something really powerful – 'No one who has faith in me will stay in the dark':

In a loud voice **Jesus** said:

Everyone who has **faith** in me also has

faith in the one who sent me.

And everyone who has seen me has seen
the one who sent me. **I am the light
that has come into the world**. No one
who has faith in me will stay in the dark.
I am not the one who will judge
those who refuse to obey my teachings.
I came to save the people of this world,
not to be their judge. But everyone
who rejects me and my teachings
will be judged on the last day by
what I have said.
John 12: 44-48 CEV

*In Him was life, and the life was the
light of men. And the light shines in
the darkness, and the darkness did not
comprehend it.*
John 1:4-5 NKJV

LIGHT IN THE DARKNESS

The light shines in the darkness,

and the darkness has not overcome it.

John 1: 5 ESV

This second translation says the darkness has not overcome the light. God's light will win.

So be encouraged to be the light in the darkness to those around you and share the good news found in God's Word.

"You are the light of the world.

A city located on a hill can't be hidden."

Matthew 5:14 WEB

Just like the stars that shine the brightest at night, we too as sons and daughters of God can shine even brighter in darkness. The amazing fact about the stars is that they are always there during the day, but the darker it gets at night, the brighter they shine!

To shine with the light of Jesus, by sharing with others the hope that we've found in Him with, is a lifesaving way to be a bright shining ray of hope to those in need.

Arise, shine;

For your light has come!

And **the glory of the Lord** is risen

upon you.

For behold, the darkness shall

cover the earth,

And deep darkness the people;

But the Lord will arise over you,

And **His glory** will be seen upon you.

The Gentiles shall come to your **light**,

And kings to the brightness of your **rising**.

Isaiah 60: 1-3 NKJV

LIGHT IN THE DARKNESS

Look up Philippians 2:15. Write out what it says about being a shining light (or some translations say like stars)

_____

_____

_____

_____

_____

_____

_____

_____

_____

Describe here or draw on the next page what being Jesus' light in the darkness means to you:

_____

_____

_____

_____

_____

_____

_____

_____

_____

LIGHT IN THE DARKNESS

What does 'staying in the light' mean to you?

_____

_____

_____

_____

_____

_____

_____

_____

_____

_____

_____

_____

_____

_____

_____

_____

_____

_____

_____

_____

_____

Has someone shone a light of hope for you before? If so, describe how God has helped you through another person:

_____

_____

_____

_____

_____

_____

_____

_____

_____

_____

_____

_____

_____

_____

_____

_____

_____

_____

_____

_____

LIGHT IN THE DARKNESS

Write out any further thoughts, prayers and verses about light in the darkness:

_____

_____

_____

_____

_____

_____

_____

_____

_____

_____

_____

_____

_____

_____

_____

_____

_____

_____

_____

_____

_____

_____

Safety

You are safe. Just like the powerful promises in Psalm 91 about God's sheltering protection, there's tremendous power in the name and blood of Jesus over this situation to protect you and your family.

During this pandemic, I've been reminded of the Passover story in Exodus chapter 12 where the blood of the lamb over the Israelites' doorposts protected them when the angel of death swept through that night. In Jesus, your household is protected by His blood.

Be encouraged to take communion, and declare over your household and all those in it that they are protected by the blood of the unblemished lamb – our Lord Jesus. Plead the blood of Jesus over your own doorpost, anoint your entranceways with oil and trust the Holy Spirit has a fortress of protection over your house.

As you go to sleep at night, don't let fearful thoughts grip your mind about what the future holds. Know God's peace and protection is in place, as the Bible says not to worry.

I will both lie down in **peace**, and sleep;

For You alone, O Lord, make me

dwell in safety.

Psalm 4: 8 NKJV

But you, O Lord, are **a shield**

around me; you are my glory, the one

who holds my head high.

I cried out to the Lord, and he

answered me from his holy mountain.

I lay down and slept, yet I woke

up in safety, for the Lord was

watching over me.

Psalm 3: 3 - 5 NLT

In any situation, we can trust that we are surely safe in God.

Recently, my daughter was a competitive gymnast who made it to a senior competition level. When gymnasts are first learning a new skill, it can seem too impossible at first, especially doing skills like backflips on a beam! And the higher level you go, the scarier the gymnastics skills can become to complete safely.

I remember when my daughter was younger and started participating in competitions. She would naturally get nervous before each competition and would sometimes say 'But what if I fall?' My immediate response the Lord gave me to say was, 'But what if you don't.'

We would pray and recite Bible verses before she went out to compete, so she knew she could trust in God for safety and having fun while out on the competition floor.

One time, while sitting on the sidelines at a competition, I had a vision as my daughter was about to compete on the beam apparatus. It was of the Lord beside her, holding her hand as she was going along the beam. It was a wonderful assurance that she wasn't alone, and that the Holy Spirit was right there with her.

She went on to complete her routine well without falling off, and winning first place! Praise the Lord!

This is such an awesome example that even though we can't always see God there at times, He is most certainly with us and gives us angels to guard us too. Throughout her competition season, she made it to a high level for years without falling off the apparatuses during competition events, which was very rare for the beam apparatus especially.

Then, at a higher level, she did fall off the beam occasionally but was never injured or fell in any way that meant she couldn't quickly stand back up and keep going. Isn't the Lord amazing!

Let's give God all the glory for His assurances and coming through with His promises of safety and protection.

> Don't be afraid, for I am with you.
>
> Don't be discouraged, for I am your God.
>
> I will strengthen you and help you.
>
> I will hold you up with my victorious
>
> right hand.
>
> Isaiah 41:10 NLT

But let all who take refuge in you rejoice;

let them ever sing for joy, and spread

your protection over them, that those

who love your name may exult in you.

For you bless the righteous, O Lord;

you cover him with favor as with

a shield.

Psalm 5: 11 - 12 ESV

This is an amazing Psalm above that promises God's protection, and also mentions rejoicing in His refuge and singing for joy while in His sheltering protection. It shows God's heart, in wanting us to live singing for joy, and not to be downcast.

In the midst of this pandemic, when the bad news seems endless, it might seem strange to feel joy or to be glad at times, but it's okay.

As Jesus says in the Bible that He came to give you life and enjoy it, God wants to bring you moments of joy and happiness, such as appreciating precious, quality time with family, friends and loved ones, as this will help you to get through the tough times.

Faith Over Fear

I came that they may have and enjoy life,

and have it in **abundance** (to the full, till

it overflows).

John 10: 10b AMPC

We can wholly trust in God's Word that says God cares for us and to not worry. Rejoice – you are safe in the power of the precious and almighty Holy Spirit who is right there with you.

God cares for you, so turn all

your worries over to him.

1 Peter 5:7 CEV

SAFETY

Has there ever been a time when you've worried about your safety?

_____

_____

_____

_____

_____

_____

_____

_____

Have these verses helped to bring assurance about safety that we have in God?

_____

_____

_____

_____

_____

_____

_____

_____

_____

But seek first the kingdom of God

and His righteousness, and all these

things shall be added to you. Therefore

do not worry about tomorrow,

for tomorrow will worry about its

own things. Sufficient for the day *is*

its own trouble.

Matthew 6: 33-34 NKJV

As you trust in God for His supernatural protection for you and your family's safety, there's an amazing peace beyond understanding that He gives us.

Jesus doesn't want our hearts to be troubled, as He said to His disciples:

Peace I leave with you, my peace

I give unto you: not as the world giveth,

give I unto you. Let not your heart

be troubled, neither let it be afraid.

John 14: 27 KJV

What verse in this chapter stands out to you the most?
Write this out in your favourite Bible translation and
note what resonates about this verse:

_____

_____

_____

_____

_____

_____

_____

_____

_____

_____

_____

_____

_____

_____

_____

_____

_____

_____

_____

Journal any other thoughts, prayers and verses about feeling **safe** in God:

_____

_____

_____

_____

_____

_____

_____

_____

_____

_____

_____

_____

_____

_____

_____

_____

_____

_____

_____

_____

_____

_____

_____

SAFETY

_____

_____

_____

_____

_____

_____

_____

_____

_____

_____

_____

_____

_____

_____

_____

_____

_____

_____

_____

_____

_____

_____

It can help at times to step away from being surrounded by the goings on of the pandemic, and take a moment to catch a heavenly perspective instead. By seeing things from a different perspective, you can rest in God and trust that He's got this. Receiving a new perspective can be like a fresh breath of heavenly wind to refresh you.

Here are some wonderful verses about trusting in the Lord:

Those who **trust in the Lord** are like Mount Zion, which cannot be moved but stands forever. The Lord is around His people like the mountains are around Jerusalem, **now and forever.**

Psalm 125: 1-2 NLV

Faith Over Fear

Cause me to hear Your lovingkindness
in the morning, For in You do I trust;
Cause me to know the way in which I
should walk, For I lift up my soul to You.

Psalm 143: 8 NKJV

Trust in the Lord with all your heart,
And lean not on your own understanding;
In all your ways acknowledge Him,
And He shall direct your paths.

Proverbs 3: 5-6 NKJV

I have kept away from the paths of the
destroyer. Uphold my steps in Your
paths, *That* my footsteps may not slip.
I have called upon You, for You will
hear me, O God; Incline Your ear to
me, *and* hear my speech.
Show Your marvelous lovingkindness
by Your right hand,

O You who save those who trust *in You*

From those who rise up *against them.*

Psalm 17: 4b – 7 NKJV

I will say of the LORD, "He is my refuge

and my fortress; my God, in Him

will I trust."

Psalm 91:2 KJ21

Something I love to do, is going for a walk near the ocean. When I look out and see how wide, how vast and can only image how deep the ocean is, it reminds me of how big God truly is. It can help put things in perspective, that God is a big God, no problem is too big for Him, and God can truly take care of everywhere for us. He is God almighty!

When we look to God as a God who is sovereign, who truly holds the world in His hands, and is mighty to save, we can get a glimpse of the bigger picture and a different perspective – that He is the ultimate One in control. We can look with a heavenly perspective to the things which are unseen:

> *So we do not lose heart.* Though our outer self
> is wasting away, our inner self is being
> renewed day by day. For this light momentary
> affliction is preparing for us an eternal weight
> of glory beyond all comparison, as we look not
> to the things that are seen but to the things
> that are unseen. *For the things that are seen are*
> *transient, but the things that are unseen are eternal.*
> 2 Corinthians 4:16-18 ESV

We can trust God when we know what type of God He is – a good, compassionate, almighty, omnipresent, righteous and loving God who fiercely loves you!

Recently, as I was sitting next to my cat, a revelation sprung to mind about trusting in God...

My cat is very timid, and when other people come around she runs and hides. But when it's just me and a friend or couple of our family members here, she's happy to say hi, happily runs to us when we call and even plays confidently with her toys like a little kitten roaring about.

She knows us, and trusts us when we're here, as she's spent long enough with us to know that she can trust that we'll look after her, give her lots of pats and that she's safe when we're around.

In the same way, we can trust God because we know that He's safe to be with. And the deeper our relationship becomes in God, the more we can instinctively trust Him, as He's with us, so there's nothing to fear.

Jesus talks about trusting who to follow in the book of John, about God being a True Shepherd and that His sheep follow Him because they know their shepherd's voice.

"The gatekeeper opens the gate for him, and the sheep listen to his voice. He calls his own sheep by name, and leads them out. Whenever he brings out his own sheep, he goes before them, and the sheep follow him, for they know his voice. They will by no means follow a stranger, but will flee from him; for they don't know the voice of strangers."

John 10: 3-5 WEB

Jesus mentions this again further along in the same chapter 10 in verses 27-28, and gives an assuring promise about not being able to be snatched from His hand:

"My sheep hear My voice, and I know them,

and they follow Me. And I give them

eternal life, and they shall never perish;

neither shall anyone snatch them out

of My hand." (NKJV)

In a pandemic where there is a lot of information to look into, it can be hard to decipher what is true, especially when there are many voices and differing views.

The sure One we can trust in is Jesus who is truth:

Jesus said to him, "I am the way,

the truth, and the life.

No one comes to the

Father except through Me.

John 14: 6 NKJV

God is the trustworthy God of Life

The Bible says Jesus is the Bread of Life that gives life to the world. It sure feels like the world is in need of God to breathe through it mightily right now to revive, heal and set many things right.

Let's pray for anyone in despair, for God to bring comfort and assurance to God's people, to build strength as their strong faith muscles begin to become flexed in the trusting. That minds become awakened with heavenly perspective, and that their eyes start shining bright with love and hope in Jesus.

Then Jesus said to them, "Most assuredly,
I say to you, Moses did not give you the bread
from heaven, but **My Father gives you the true
bread from heaven.** For the bread of God is He
who comes down from **heaven** and gives
life to the world."
Then they said to Him, "Lord, give us
this bread always."
And Jesus said to them, "I am the bread of
life. He who comes to Me shall never hunger,
and he who **believes in Me** shall never thirst.
John 6: 32 - 35 NKJV

God wants to give you eternal living water, life!

Jesus said to her, "Everyone who drinks of
this water will be thirsty again, but
whoever drinks of the water that I
will give him will never be thirsty
again. The water that I will give
him will become in him a spring of
water welling up to eternal life.

John 4: 13-14 ESV

Coming to Jesus and drinking of His living water
is an amazing gift of His grace.

*In God you'll find unconditional love and
grace and you can trust in how much He
loves you.*

You can trust in how much He cares. You can
trust God for all your provisions. You can trust in
the good Lord for everything you need physically,
mentally and spiritually. You can trust in His
unfailing love for you.

TRUST

So we have come to know and trust in
the love that God has for us. God is love.
Now whoever abides in love abides in God,
and God abides in him.

1 John 4:16 TLV

I am God! I can be trusted.
Your past troubles are gone;
I no longer think of them.
When you pray for someone
to receive a blessing,
or when you make a promise,
you must do it in my name.
I alone am the God
who can be trusted.

Isaiah 65: 16 CEV

The LORD *is* gracious and full of compassion,

Slow to anger and great in mercy.

The LORD *is* good to all,

And His tender mercies *are* over all

His works.

Psalm 145: 8-9 NKJV

Trusting in God can come in different ways. We can trust God to safely get us places when we travel. We can trust God to guide us on the right paths of life. We can trust God for provision for everything we need, even when it looks like circumstances say otherwise.

When I first became a Christian, I was so fascinated learning about the supernatural (and I'm still fascinated today as there's still so much to learn!)

There was a whole other spiritual realm that I learnt existed, and I was newly learning about a God that was mind-blowingly amazing; a God who performed miracles, supernaturally intervened in situations, was in control of the weather and the whole earth, and gave us angels to protect us.

That God was and is able to do anything.

I loved hearing stories from fellow Christians of miracles, angels in disguise turning up to help stranded people, petrol gauges supernaturally rising right before people's eyes, a friend seeing angels light up while walking home in the dark, healings where people's uneven legs would grow, people getting out of wheelchairs and sickness' being immediately healed by the Holy Spirit.

This became and now still is my new normal. I began to experience supernatural healing and miracles too, and quickly learned early on that nothing is impossible for God.

with God nothing shall be impossible

Luke 1: 37 KJV

Recently, the Lord showed me something that pictured what living and trusting in Him so we can enjoy our lives looks like.

It was a vision, imaginaing a family going on holiday, with everything already paid for, so they could just go along and enjoy it. They didn't have to worry about the cost when it came to choosing their activities and travel plans as it was all already paid for. The same way, Jesus has already paid the price by dying on the cross for our salvation and everything we need, so we can live set free in Him. By living in Him there's nothing to worry about – God has already set out good plans for your life and already has everything covered.

As I was thinking about the ways that God provides, I was reminded of hearing two stories, years ago, that were quite similar. In both stories, a couple were having people over for a meal but didn't have enough for everyone. In one story, the husband ended up inviting more people over, so the wife was stressing a lot. They only had one chicken to feed many.

But they prayed and trusted in God, and literally watched as God provided miraculously, and also multiplied their food as the food plate was being passed around, so there was more than enough. I love hearing stories like these!

I'm also in wonder of nature and how God created plants and their fruit to provide by naturally multiplying.

Like a tomato, that has many seeds within, and every one of those seeds can become an entire new plant that can grow many more tomatoes. And not only that – each one of those tomatoes also has many more seeds! I think this is incredible multiplication that God has created!

The Bible says in the Gospels that twice Jesus miraculously provided for thousands of people that came to see Him, by multiplying a small amount of food. Both times Jesus multiplied a few loaves and fish into much!

He gave thanks, blessed the food, then broke the bread before the disciples passed it around. The multitude of people ate and were satisfied! And not just that – there were baskets full of leftovers!

It's in times like these, that can be an opportunity to stir our faith and be reminded that our faith needs to be founded in God and not in man.

If you are waiting for God's provisions during this pandemic, due to the shortages of supplies or delays that has come from it, then be encouraged today that God knows and already has a solution for you and your loved ones.

There is something special that can happen in the waiting and trusting in the Lord. We can draw closer to God during this time and learn from Him, hear what He might want to say along the journey, and rest in the revelation that He truly is an almighty God. He's got this, and will *always* come through for you! You can trust in Him.

Faith Over Fear

I trust the Lord God
to save me,
and I will wait for him
to answer my prayer.

Micah 7:7 CEV

Our lives here on earth can seem fleeting, before going to our heavenly home for all of eternity, but we can trust in God because He's always with us. The NLT translation talks about God's love remaining with us and our family's generations to come after us:

But the love of the Lord remains forever
with those who fear him.
His salvation extends to the children's
children of those who are faithful
to his covenant, of those who obey his
commandments!
The Lord has made the heavens his
throne; from there he rules
over everything.

Psalm 103:17-19 NLT

This amazing Psalm also exalts God for who He is, and reminds us that it is He who is the creator of the heavens and earth and rules over everything, and the Lord's love remains with us forever.

We can trust in the love of God.

Lately, I have felt to take breaks from watching mainstream news where possible, and it has helped a lot with having the peace of God guide my thoughts.

I have been reminded of this next verse a lot, and I hope it will encourage you also to focus on things above, and on what God might want to say and display through the darkness.

As mentioned in the chapter Peace also, these scriptures give awseome direction for what types of things to think on:

'Whatever is true, whatever is honorable,

whatever is just, whatever is pure,

whatever is lovely, whatever is commendable—

if there is any virtue and if there is anything

worthy of praise—dwell on these things'

Philippians 4:8 TLV

Faith Over Fear

Praise the LORD.
Blessed are those who fear the LORD,
who find great delight in his commands.
Their children will be mighty in the land;
the generation of the upright will be blessed.
Wealth and riches are in their houses,
and their righteousness endures forever.
Even in darkness light dawns for the upright,
for those who are gracious and compassionate
and righteous.
Good will come to those who are generous
and lend freely,
who conduct their affairs with justice.
Surely the righteous will never be shaken;
they will be remembered forever.
They will have no fear of bad news;
their hearts are steadfast, trusting in the LORD.
Their hearts are secure, they will have no fear;
in the end they will look in triumph on their foes.
They have freely scattered their gifts to the poor,
their righteousness endures forever;
their horn will be lifted high in honor.

Psalm 112: 1-9 NIV

What do think God's perspective is during these times?

_____

_____

_____

_____

_____

_____

_____

_____

_____

_____

_____

_____

_____

_____

_____

_____

_____

_____

_____

_____

_____

_____

_____

God turns all things for good for those that love Him
(Romans 8:28). Can you picture or imagine how He
could do this in your situation?

_____

_____

_____

_____

_____

_____

_____

_____

_____

_____

_____

_____

_____

_____

_____

_____

_____

_____

_____

What does 'thinking with a heavenly perspective' look like to you?

_____

_____

_____

_____

_____

_____

_____

_____

_____

_____

_____

_____

_____

_____

_____

_____

_____

_____

_____

Does this help you to trust more in God?

_____

_____

_____

_____

_____

What verse from this chapter stands out to you the most and why?

_____

_____

_____

_____

_____

_____

_____

_____

_____

_____

_____

_____

_____

TRUST

In what ways big or small can we trust in God:

_____

_____

_____

_____

_____

_____

_____

_____

_____

_____

_____

_____

_____

_____

_____

_____

_____

_____

_____

_____

_____

Journal any other thoughts, prayers and verses about **trusting** in God:

_____

_____

_____

_____

_____

_____

_____

_____

_____

_____

_____

_____

_____

_____

_____

_____

_____

_____

_____

_____

_____

TRUST

_____

_____

_____

_____

_____

_____

_____

_____

_____

_____

_____

_____

_____

_____

_____

_____

_____

_____

_____

_____

_____

_____

The LORD is my light and my salvation; whom shall I fear? the LORD is the strength of my life; of whom shall I be afraid?

I had fainted, unless I had believed to see the goodness of the LORD in the land of the living.

Wait on the LORD: be of good courage, and he shall strengthen thine heart: wait, I say, on the LORD.

Psalm 27: 1 & 7-8 KJV

Strength

"Do not sorrow, for the

joy of the LORD is your strength."

Nehemiah 8: 10c NKJV

There is tremendous strength in trusting in the power of God.

If you happen to feel anxious about going out and about during the pandemic, don't panic or give in to fear.

Instead, trust in God's protection over your life. Remember what it says in Psalm 91; that no harm shall come near you. His angels are guarding you, and we have the most powerful Protector, the precious Holy Spirit who is right here with us.

No enemy can break through God's supernatural

protective barrier.

We can be encouraged by what God said to Joshua, when they were about to cross over into the promised land, in the face of giants:

> This is my command—be strong
> and courageous! Do not be afraid
> or discouraged. **For the Lord
> your God is with you** wherever
> you go."
> Joshua 1:9 NLT

God is with us!

Here are some more encouraging verses to build your faith muscles in God's strength:

> I can do all things because Christ
> gives me the strength.
> Philippians 4:13 NLV

> No weapon that is formed against
> you will prevail.
> Isaiah 54: 17a WEB

The Contemporary English Version says:

> Weapons made to attack you
> won't be successful;
> words spoken against you
> won't hurt at all.
> Isaiah 54: 17 CEV

Did you know that prayer is incredibly powerful! Especially in these times where you might be wondering what to do – be encouraged to draw strength from God by praying and releasing your requests into His hands.

> The prayer of **faith** will save the one who
> is sick, and **the Lord will raise him up.**
> If he has committed sins, he will
> be forgiven.
> James 5: 15 TLV

> The earnest **prayer** of a **righteous** person
> has great **power** and produces
> wonderful results.
> James 5: 16b NLT

I was thinking about being prepared during this pandemic as the Lord showed me an example of how parents prepare for their children during the start of a school year.

Before children start a new school year, parents rush around making sure their children have everything they need; school uniforms, school books and stationary, a backpack and lunchboxes ready to go. They don't want their children to be unprepared, nor not have anything to eat at lunchtime, as starting a new school year without those things would be quite stressful for them.

In the same way, before we go out to face the day's challenges, how much more does God as a loving Heavenly Father have everything that we need pre-prepared for us. Even if you can't see something yet, trust in Him that what you need is on its way in God's perfect timing.

As well as all our provisions that we need, God has also quipped us with the Bible, the trusted Words of God, and the armour of God.

To take a stand over fear, let's see what God's armour that He clothes His people in looks like for taking up faith-filled courage. The next verse is particularly encouraging about being strong in the Lord and in the strength of His might!

STRENGTH

Finally, be strong in the Lord and in the strength of his might. Put on the whole armor of God, that you may be able to stand against the schemes of the devil. For we do not wrestle against flesh and blood, but against the rulers, against the authorities, against the cosmic powers over this present darkness, against the spiritual forces of evil in the heavenly places. Therefore take up the whole armor of God, that you may be able to withstand in the evil day, and having done all, to stand firm. Stand therefore, having fastened on the belt of truth, and having put on the breastplate of righteousness, and, as shoes for your feet, having put on the readiness given by the gospel of peace. In all circumstances take up the shield of faith, with which you can extinguish all the flaming darts of the evil one; and take the helmet of salvation, and the sword of the Spirit, which is the word of God, praying at all times in the Spirit, with all prayer and supplication. To that end, keep alert with all perseverance, making supplication for all the saints.

Ephesians 6:10-18 ESV

Now that we're aware of the armour we have, we don't need to try and fight this situation on our own or by our own strengths.

There's something really powerful about fasting too. If you have ever fasted in God, you may have experienced something incredible. In the first period of time it can be hard as you're wrestling with your hunger, but then when you slip into God's supernatural strength it feels amazing! I have experienced the supernatural strength of God come upon me several times, not only when fasting, and you just know that it's God – feeling the incredible power and presence of the Holy Spirit that's with you.

Have you never heard?

Have you never understood?

The LORD is the everlasting God,

the Creator of all the earth.

He never grows weak or weary.

No one can measure the depths of

his understanding.

He gives power to the weak

and strength to the powerless.

Even youths will become weak and tired,

and young men will fall in exhaustion.

But those who trust in the
LORD will find new strength.

They will soar high on wings like eagles.

They will run and not grow weary.

They will walk and not faint.

Isaiah 40: 28-31 NLT

"The Lord himself will fight for you.

Just stay calm."

Exodus 14:14 NLT

I love this next verse in Timothy - 'Fight the good fight of faith'. It seems fitting to include in a book about faith! Holding onto your faith and pursing all good things can seem like a fight, especially when the enemy wants you to cower in fear.

Pursue righteousness, godliness, faith,
love, steadfastness, gentleness. Fight
the good fight of the faith. Take hold
of the eternal life to which you were

called and about which you made the good

confession in the presence of many witnesses.

1 Timothy 6: 11b – 12 ESV

In this time of uncertainty where circumstances can feel beyond us, we can lean into God for His grace and strength. Know that God is scooping you up in His arms at this time and shielding you with His protection. When we are weak *He* is strong.

Each time he said, "**My grace is all you need**.

My power works best in weakness."

So now I am glad to boast about my

weaknesses, so that the power of **Christ**

can work through me.

2 Corinthians 12: 9 NLT

When we have resilience in our faith in God, our hope in Him strengthens.

Psalm 84 talks about happiness in relation to strength in God:

How happy is the man whose strength

is in You and in whose heart are the

roads to Zion!

Psalm 84: 5 NLV

Another translation in the NKJV says blessed:

Blessed *is* the man whose strength *is* in You,

Whose heart *is* set on pilgrimage.

This verse has so much to it in only two lines. Blessed are you when you put your strength in God is the first part. And then the second part, still within the same sentence, talks about a journey. A pilgrim is a person on a journey with spiritual significance. As we journey through this pandemic, we can discover new things not ever dreamed of before along the way.

Our faith can seem like it might be shattered with fear in certain circumstances. But I'm so thankful we serve a God who works all things for good. We can come out strongly in our faith in God, and hold on to see Him do great things in the midst! What might be the miracle that's just around the corner!

For the eyes of the LORD run to and

fro throughout the whole earth, to show

Himself strong on behalf of *those* whose

heart *is* loyal to Him.

2 Chronicles 16:9a NKJV

Here are some more encouraging verses about being strong in the Lord. The first, a prayer by Paul in Ephesians and a few more incredible verses about strength in rest, and that our strength comes from the Lord:

That He would grant you, according to

the riches of His glory, to be strengthened

with might by His Spirit in the

inner man; that Christ may dwell in

your hearts by faith.

Ephesians 3: 16-17a KJ21

"In returning and rest you shall be saved;

In quietness and confidence shall be

your strength."

Isaiah 30 :15 NKJV

STRENGTH

Yet the Lord is faithful, and He will
strengthen [you] *and* set you on a
firm foundation and guard you
from the evil [one].

2 Thessalonians 3:3 AMPC

"Behold, God is my salvation;
I will trust, and will not be afraid;
for the Lord God is my strength and
my song, and he has become my salvation."

Isaiah 12: 2 ESV

Fear not, for I *am* with you;
Be not dismayed, for I *am* your God.
I will strengthen you, Yes, I will help you,
I will uphold you with My righteous
right hand.'

Isaiah 41:10 NKJV

Note a verse from this chapter about strength that stood out to you the most, and why:

_____

_____

_____

_____

_____

_____

_____

_____

_____

_____

_____

_____

_____

_____

_____

_____

_____

_____

_____

_____

_____

STRENGTH

DECLARATIONS OF FAITH TO GIVE YOU STRENGTH IN GOD

1. We can have faith in God because He Himself is faithful.

2. **We can trust in God, because He Himself is trustworthy.**

3. We can love God, because He Himself first loved us, and sent His one and only Son to die on a cross for us.

4. We can find grace in God, because He Himself is the person of grace.

5. We can find strength in God, because He Himself is strong.

Rewrite the same faith declarations, changing the word 'we' to 'I', and 'us' to 'me', to make it a personal declaration over your life. For example: '*I can find strength in God because He Himself is strong.*'

_____

_____

_____

_____

_____

_____

_____

_____

_____

_____

_____

_____

_____

_____

_____

_____

_____

_____

_____

_____

Faith Over Fear

What does being strong in the Lord look like or feel like to you?

_____

_____

_____

_____

_____

_____

_____

_____

_____

_____

_____

_____

_____

_____

_____

_____

_____

_____

_____

_____

_____

Write out your own thoughts, prayers and other verses about **strength** in God:

_____

_____

_____

_____

_____

_____

_____

_____

_____

_____

_____

_____

_____

_____

_____

_____

_____

_____

_____

_____

_____

_____

STRENGTH

_____

_____

_____

_____

_____

_____

_____

_____

_____

_____

_____

_____

_____

_____

_____

_____

_____

_____

_____

_____

_____

_____

Our soul waits for the Lord.

He is our help and our safe cover.

For *our heart is full of joy in Him*,

because we trust in His holy name.

O Lord, let Your loving-kindness

be upon us as we put our

hope in You.

Psalm 33: 20-22 NLV

Hope

Having hope is so beautiful. It lifts us up. Even if we catch just a glimmer of hope – it's enough to spur us on and let God's light in to guide our path.

Hope deferred maketh the heart sick:

but when the desire cometh, it is a

tree of life.

Proverbs 13:12 KJV

We put our **hope** in the LORD.
He is our help and our shield.

Psalm 33: 20 NLT

When we look through the lens of fear, our outlook becomes blurred as we become worried and anxious, or begin leaning on the thought train of 'what ifs' – consumed by fear about bad things that could happen.

But looking through the lens of hope gives you a positive outlook and powerful resolution of truth found in God and in His perspective.

> There is surely a future hope for you,
>
> and your hope will not be cut off.

Proverbs 23:18 NIV

> Because of the LORD's great love we
>
> are not consumed, for his compassions
>
> never fail. They are new every morning;
>
> great is your faithfulness.
>
> I say to myself, "The LORD is my portion;
>
> therefore I will wait for him."
>
> The LORD is good to those whose hope
>
> is in him, to the one who seeks him;
>
> it is good to wait quietly for the salvation
>
> of the LORD.

Lamentations 3: 22 – 26 NIV

A joyful heart is good medicine,

but a crushed spirit dries up the bones.

Proverbs 17: 22 ESV

Therefore, having been justified by faith,
we have peace with God through our Lord
Jesus Christ, through whom also we have
access by faith into this grace in which we
stand, and rejoice in hope of the glory
of God. And not only *that*, but we also
glory in tribulations, knowing that tribulation
produces perseverance; and perseverance,
character; and character, hope.
Now hope does not disappoint, because
the love of God has been poured out in
our hearts by the Holy Spirit who was
given to us.

Romans 5: 1 - 5 NKJV

God's Hope Shining Through Kindness

Kindness is something that is incredibly powerful,
and can go hand-in-hand with hope. Hearing
stories and seeing acts of kindness everywhere

helps to burst this darkness with God's light and love in people's hearts, to encourage them to find hope again.

Here is a verse from the Bible where Jesus encourages His people to love one another:

"A new commandment I give to you, that
you love one another: just as I have loved
you, you also are to love one another.
By this all people will know that you
are my disciples, if you have love
for one another."
John 13: 34-35 ESV

Therefore, we who have fled to him for
refuge can have great confidence as we
hold to the hope that lies before us. This
hope is a strong and trustworthy anchor
for our souls. It leads us through the curtain
into God's inner sanctuary. Jesus has
already gone in there for us.
Hebrews 6: 18b – 20a NLT

I wait for the **Lord**. My soul waits and
I hope in **His Word**. My **soul** waits for
the **Lord** more than one who watches
for the morning; yes, more than one who
watches for the morning. O Israel,
hope in the Lord! For there is
loving-kindness with the Lord. With
Him we are **saved** for sure.

Psalm 130: 5-7 NLV

Earlier in the book, I'd mentioned faith playing a roll in our lives like a board game, and promised to let you know what game piece tool I'd choose in this moment in time.

Imagine a large board game spread out before you like a map. You move your awesome main game piece (that's you) forward and see what the next challenge says in that spot.

In this pandemic it can seem like there are more bad challenges to overcome versus bonus good spots to land on. But God hasn't left us out there alone in the game, instead He's given us a tool kit filled with many options to choose from.

And, if we look at the map from a higher vantage point, we'll also see many other bright shining lights – other Christians that God has placed around us for fellowship, and to pray and journey together with.

As each obstacle or challenge comes our way, we can look into a treasure chest type of tool kit that's with us, and choose something to respond with for each circumstance.

We can choose one or many of these like:

> **Hope in God** when things look dark,
>
> **trusting in God** when things looks unstable,
>
> **grace** when we need His grace,
>
> **love** to respond with,
>
> **forgiveness** for unkindness,
>
> **compassion** for those hurting,
>
> **patience** when waiting for an outcome,
>
> standing up for our **freedom** in Christ,
>
> **faith** in God for the situation,
>
> **truth** when presented with lies,
>
> and even things like **resolution** and
>
> **determination** to stay the course with God.

For though we walk in the flesh, we do
not war after the flesh:
(For the weapons of our warfare are not
carnal, but mighty through God to the
pulling down of strong holds;)
Casting down imaginations, and every
high thing that exalteth itself against the
knowledge of God, and bringing into
captivity every thought to the obedience
of Christ.

2 Corinthians 10: 3-5 KJV

You might be able to guess what my 'game piece' choice is, given that we're in the chapter titled Hope, which is correct! It's what's standing out like a shining beacon for me right now.

In light of current circumstances around the world, where it sounds like there's more crisis on the way, I have been feeling the weight of all that's happening, and honestly I feel like it would be easier if everyone would just play nicely in the playground and get along. Reading news articles is wise to find out what's happening, but I noticed that I was becoming more and more aware of the bad effect that bad news was having on me, causing stress. I was continually seeing all the bad reports of what the devil was stirring up without balance in my thinking.

God began to show me that what was missing in how I was thinking about everything was looking to God more for how He was going to move in these circumstances. Instead of being consumed by the bad, I'm choosing to look to God and have *hope. Hope in Him*, not in myself to try and get through, but in the grace of God for all the good things He's doing and about to do.

Since then, as I've looked to God in faith, trusting that He truly is going to take care of us and do great things in the earth in the midst of this darkness, God has given me some amazing visions! Prophetic visions of good things that are coming too!

I've received many recently, too many to yet pen, but one comes to mind that I'd like to share. It was of the greatest outpouring from heaven! The colour was like a white-silver, which I always see as the Spirit of God, and it was pouring tremendously as a heavenly watering for souls all over the earth.

It has made me think on how big God really is, and how truly magnificent what He's about to do is!

"Thus says the LORD who made it, the
LORD who formed it to establish it
(the LORD *is* His name): 'Call to Me,
and I will answer you, and show you
great and mighty things, which you
do not know.'
Jeremiah 33: 2-3 NKJV

So today, I'm choosing *hope* in the wonderful Lord Jesus.

I'm curious what is standing out for you today to walk in or pick up in the face of your current situation. There's a question in the journal section coming up that you can note soon.

Let's be aware that the enemy also has tools that he'd like you to pick up. In response to a bad situation – fear, anxiety, despair, striving in our own strength to try and fix everything, depression, cowering away, unrelenting anger or a feeling of hopelessness might try to appear in your toolbox. It might look like something that will aid you to 'get through' and seem easier to respond with to evil circumstances.

But what the enemy, the devil, throws at us is

always counterfeit to God. It doesn't bring life, but instead is deceptive to try to destroy us and stop us moving forward on the map of life. Jesus said: The thief does not come except to steal, and to kill, and to destroy. I have come that they may have life, and that they may have *it* more abundantly. (John 10: 10 NKJV)

Let's not let our game piece tools fall to the ground and get covered in the dust where we might not see them there as clearly. Instead, let's walk in love, hope and light in Jesus, and trustingly let Him lead us along right and lifegiving paths.

If you are finding it hard to have faith, don't worry, you can ask God to help you give you strength to have faith and hope in Him.

God is always in the 'and then'. As situations appear, there's always an 'and then God' response, as He doesn't leave His children hanging or waiting in the dark, but comes through with a response, a solution and restoration.

He knows it's a struggle in these tough times, but you can trust He's going to answer your requests and prayers. Like the verse above in Jeremiah, God says to call to Him and He will answer you.

In Isaiah 65: 17-25, Isaiah is prophesying about a new heaven and a new earth. In verse 24, God says He will answer prayers before they are even finished speaking! We can have hope for the new to come, where there will be no more weeping or crying in distress, but instead there will be joy.

"For behold, I create new heavens and a

new earth, and the former things shall not be

remembered or come into mind.

But be glad and rejoice forever in that which

I create; for behold, I create Jerusalem

to be a joy, and her people to be a gladness.

I will rejoice in Jerusalem and be glad in

my people; no more shall be heard in

it the sound of weeping and the cry of distress.

No more shall there be in it an infant who

lives but a few days, or an old man who

does not fill out his days, for the young man

shall die a hundred years old, and the

sinner a hundred years old shall be accursed.

They shall build houses and inhabit them;

Faith Over Fear

they shall plant vineyards and eat their fruit.

They shall not build and another inhabit;

they shall not plant and another eat;

for like the days of a tree shall the days

of my people be, and my chosen shall long

enjoy the work of their hands.

They shall not labor in vain or bear

children for calamity, for they shall be the

offspring of the blessed of the LORD,

and their descendants with them.

Before they call I will answer;

while they are yet speaking I will hear.

The wolf and the lamb shall graze together;

the lion shall eat straw like the ox,

and dust shall be the serpent's food.

They shall not hurt or destroy in all

my holy mountain," says the LORD. (ESV)

As children of the Light, we have such tremendous supernatural favour that's on our side in Jesus. There's power in our prayers to see miracles happen, and 'bonus' game options will appear even if it seems impossible.

In Jesus, you are blessed with every spiritual blessing:

Grace and *shalom* to you, from God
our Father and the Lord *Yeshua* the Messiah!
Blessed be the God and Father of our
Lord *Yeshua* the Messiah, who has blessed
us with every spiritual blessing in the
heavenly places in Messiah.
He chose us in the Messiah before the
foundation of the world, to be holy
and blameless before Him in love.
He predestined us for adoption as
sons through Messiah *Yeshua*, in keeping
with the good pleasure of His will.
Ephesians 1: 2-5 TLV

Having hope in God is like receiving fresh, light wings. It's incredibly lifegiving, as a burst of hope is like faith that soars in God's healing winds lifting you up afresh!

The next verse is one of my favourite verses in the Bible.

It starts by saying that God is the God of hope! I love this. The verse is a prayer about being filled with joy and peace in believing, and abounding in hope by the power of the Holy Spirit.

Now may **the God of hope** fill you with all

joy and **peace** in believing, that you may

abound in **hope**, in the **power of the Holy Spirit**.

Romans 15: 13 WEB

As you read this I pray you'll receive a fresh in-filling of hope in God today!

May He lift up your wings with healing winds afresh in Him!

The following verse is also incredibly powerful, talking about a *living* hope and also awesomely ties in with faith.

Praise be to the God and Father of our Lord Jesus Christ! In his great mercy he has given us new birth into a living hope through the resurrection of Jesus Christ from the dead, and into an inheritance that can never perish, spoil or fade. This inheritance is kept in heaven for you, who through **faith are shielded** by **God's power** until the coming of the **salvation** that is ready to be revealed in the last time. In all this you greatly rejoice, though now for a little while you may have had to suffer grief in all kinds of trials. These have come so that the proven genuineness of your **faith**—of greater worth than gold, which perishes even though refined by fire—may result in praise, glory and honor when **Jesus Christ** is revealed. Though you have not seen him, you **love** him; and even though you do not see him now, you believe in him and are filled with an inexpressible and glorious **joy**, for you are receiving the end result of your faith, the salvation of your souls.

1 Peter 1: 3-9 NIV

Describe what having hope feels like to you?

_____

_____

_____

_____

_____

_____

_____

_____

_____

_____

_____

_____

_____

_____

_____

_____

_____

_____

_____

_____

_____

What's something in God's tool kit that you could choose to put forward in your circumstances today?

_____

_____

_____

_____

_____

_____

_____

_____

_____

_____

_____

_____

_____

_____

_____

_____

_____

_____

_____

_____

If hope was a colour, what colour would it be?

_____

_____

_____

_____

_____

Note what you're currently experiencing regarding hope:

_____

_____

_____

_____

_____

_____

_____

_____

_____

_____

_____

_____

_____

_____

HOPE

Faith Over Fear

Note any other thoughts, prayers and verses about **hope** found in God:

_____

_____

_____

_____

_____

_____

_____

_____

_____

_____

_____

_____

_____

_____

_____

_____

_____

_____

_____

_____

Healing

Let's say a prayer together if you'd like healing. It's a wonderful reminder that God is a Healer. He can heal anything miraculously and His will is for you, and not just for your physical healing but also in your spiritual and mental health also.

Remember, Jesus has already won the victory over sickness on the cross. So you can declare that in the face of fear, worry or uncertainty – you are already healed in Jesus. He has already defeated sickness on the cross – in Him you are healed, whole and set free!

Dear God

I come to You today and firstly thank you, Jesus, that You went to that cross, and by Your innocent blood that was shed, You paid the price for our healing in You.

I pray for those that are in need of a physical healing to be set free in Jesus' name. I thank you, God, for the washing of the blood of Jesus over their lives, and that they can hold onto and dwell with the Holy Spirit who is with them. Thank you, God, that in You they're already forgiven and healed through Your precious blood that washes us clean, that You have paid the price for our redemption and healing.

Thank you that You are the God of miracles and for Your tremendous, life-saving power that can lift us up out of the grave of sickness and into a place of running well in You. Thank you for miracles in every possible way for this dear reader, and that You indeed make a way, even through impossibility. There's nothing that's impossible for You, God, and I pray for everyone needing a miracle today that they'll shout for joy at seeing Your face that loves them, and Your hand that brings about the true healing they need.

I pray for anyone who's going through a relationship difficulty right now, that they would be filled with hope. I pray for fractured relationships that have come about from this pandemic to mend and heal in Jesus. Lord, may You wrap Your arms around everyone involved, and bring peace, love and unity back into those relationships. Your intention is for good, and unity, Lord, and I pray for restoration for what has been lost.

God, You care deeply about right relationships and I thank you that nothing is too impossible, too lost, or too late to mend and restore back to life and happiness again.

HEALING

For anyone struggling with the torment of fear, anxiety or depression, I pray for a deep healing from inside out and that their mind is set free in Jesus' name. That in You, God, they'll find true freedom, health to all parts of their body, mind, and spirit, and their soul would leap for joy instead of despair. I declare over you, precious reader, that despair, fear and anything trying to trap you and keep the joy of the Lord away will go and never return in Jesus' name.

Today, stand up and take a new fresh breath in God, knowing who He is – that He loves You dearly and wants you healed, whole and enjoying life in Him.

I pray, God, to breathe on the life of this dear reader afresh, as they're made whole and healed, and that they'll be set free in every area of their lives, both now and forever.

From everlasting to everlasting, may they know the depths of Your love for them, and how much You care, Oh God. Oh, that You *do* care, even more than we realise. May their eyes, hearts and souls be opened to how much You care for them in all ways as Your precious child. *Amen.*

For you who fear my name, the **Sun of Righteousness** will rise with **healing in his wings**. And you will go **free**, leaping with **joy** like calves let out to pasture.

Malachi 4:2 NLT

Look up Isaiah 61:1 and Psalm 147:3. What do these verses have in common?

_____

_____

_____

_____

_____

_____

_____

_____

_____

_____

_____

_____

_____

_____

_____

_____

_____

_____

_____

_____

_____

_____

Journal your thoughts, prayers and verses about **healing**:

_____

_____

_____

_____

_____

_____

_____

_____

_____

_____

_____

_____

_____

_____

_____

_____

_____

_____

_____

_____

_____

_____

God's Goodness

One day during lockdown, I was busy trying to remember to eat and drink the right healthy things during this time like: taking apple cider vinegar, a spoonful of raw lemon juice for vitamin C, ginger, and I had garlic on my list but it had been sold out for a while in store. But while I was pondering these things, an idea dawned on me about taking a spoonful of God's Word. Like taking a daily spoonful of God's supernatural medicine.

Rather than waking up and rushing to get through each task for the day, I was reminded about spending time in the Bible first. What a great way to set up the day with truthful, life-giving verses that sets you up on the right path for the day – being full of faith in God's protection on a daily basis, rather than being inundated with fear each time the news shares something bad that's happening.

The Bible has something amazing to say about listening to good, wise words:

For they are life to those who find them,

healing and health to all their flesh.

Proverbs 4:22 AMPC

If you're feeling like you're now growing in encouragement and faith in God's Word and His light – be encouraged to spread the light of God to others. There are so many negative reports in the news that keeps bombarding us daily, that even a little glimmer of something positive happening seems to feel quite powerful and has a tremendous effect.

If you have a neighbour or friend who just needs to hear that good can come out of this situation and that they'll be okay – that they're safe and tremendously loved by God, be encouraged to share positive words and verses with them too.

In the book of Romans it says that God works all things for good for us.

So no matter what you're going through – God can turn it around for good.

> We know that all things work together for
>
> good to them that love God, to them who
>
> are the called according to his purpose.
>
> Romans 8: 28 KJV

The Bible also encourages us that good words bring health:

> **The light of the eyes rejoices the heart,**
> ***And* a good report makes the bones healthy.**
> **Proverbs 15: 30 NKJV**

Kindness can be so impacting. God is kind to us, and it's important to be kind to others, especially those that are feeling strained by the longevity of this situation.

> Anxiety weighs down the heart,
>
> but a kind word cheers it up.
>
> Proverbs 12: 25 NIV

God is so so good. The goodness of God is like basking in warm sunshine.

Let's reflect on the Lord's goodness for a moment, and remember all the wonderful things He has done for us.

This can help us have faith that if God has come through for us and done such wonderful things before, then how much so will we see our wonderful God do good things and amazing miracles again! And let's remember to give Him thanks.

> O **give thanks to the Lord**. Call on His name.
> Make His works known among the people.
> Sing to Him. Sing **praises** to Him. Tell of
> all His great works. Honor His holy name.
> Let the heart of those who look to the Lord
> be glad. **Look for the Lord and His strength.**
> Look for His face all the time. **Remember the**
> **great and powerful works that He has done.**
> Psalm 105: 1 – 5a NLV

We can trust in God's goodness towards us, because He is a good God who takes care of us.

And how awesome is it that you'll find the letters G.O.D. in the word GOOD.

> **I am the Good Shepherd; the Good Shepherd**
>
> **giveth His life for the sheep.**
>
> **John 10: 11 KJ21**

Jesus, talking about sheep in the book of John 10, says in verse 9 that He is the way to life and those that come through Him find what they need. We serve a good God who has provided a way for us to be in relationship with Him – isn't that truly amazing.

I feel grateful to know how good God is.

> I am the Door; anyone who enters in through
>
> Me will be saved (will live). He will come in
>
> and he will go out [freely], and will find pasture.
>
> John 10: 9 AMPC

In the next verse, Jesus gives a truth-filled explanation about what the devil is like versus Himself.

In His goodness, God won't take from you, hurt or

destroy you, but instead He is the God who gives abundant life to you!

And the kind of life that Jesus gives to us through salvation in Him is everlasting!

> The thief comes only to steal, slaughter,
> and destroy. *I have come that they*
> *might have life, and have it abundantly!*
> John 10: 10 TLV

Let's praise God for being a good God, full of wonderful goodness!

> Make a joyful shout to the LORD, all
> you lands! Serve the LORD with gladness;
> Come before His presence with singing.
> Know that the LORD, He *is* God;
> *It is* He *who* has made us, and not
> we ourselves; *We are* His people and the
> sheep of His pasture.
> Enter into His gates with thanksgiving,
> *And* into His courts with praise.

Be thankful to Him, *and* bless His name. For the LORD *is* good;

His mercy *is* everlasting, And

His truth *endures* to all generations.

Psalm 100 NKJV

I have a word on my heart that I would love to share with you, dear reader. *'You are important to God'*. Your spiritual health is important to God, but all areas of your life are also important to God. Your physical health, and how your mental health and happiness is as you go through this pandemic, is important to God, and He wants to see you living well holisticaly. That's how good God is - He wants you to know how important you are to Him.

Don't let anyone or any circumstance tell you otherwise. You are important. You are valued. Your life is extremely precious to God – both now and forever!

O taste and see that the LORD is good:

blessed is the man that trusteth in him.

Psalm 34:8 KJV

Experiencing the goodness of God can start with looking at who God is as a good God. What are some of the characteristics of God that shows He is good?

_____

_____

_____

_____

_____

_____

_____

_____

_____

_____

_____

_____

_____

_____

_____

_____

_____

_____

_____

GOD'S GOODNESS

Describe how God has been good to you before:

_____

_____

_____

_____

_____

_____

_____

_____

_____

_____

_____

_____

_____

_____

_____

_____

_____

_____

_____

_____

_____

_____

Write out any other thoughts, prayers and verses about the **goodness of God**:

_____

_____

_____

_____

_____

_____

_____

_____

_____

_____

_____

_____

_____

_____

_____

_____

_____

_____

_____

_____

GOD'S GOODNESS

Peace

Peace I leave with you. My peace I give

to you; not as the world gives, I give

to you. Don't let not your heart be

troubled, neither let it be fearful.

John 14: 27 WEB

Having faith in God during these times is trusting Him to work it all out. To let go of uncertainty and let God be our rock in every circumstance. To be at peace in the trusting.

Be encouraged not to look at the news too often, and to take a break sometimes – as seeing bad news all the time can increase the feeling of fear and despair that is trying to take hold of the world in a big way.

Faith Over Fear

For God hath not given us the spirit of

fear; but of power, and of love, and

of a sound mind.

2 Timothy 1: 7 KJV

If you happen to be isolating, one good thing about staying indoors and not needing to rush about so much, is the opportunity to spend more time with God. To find peace in the resting. To hear what God might be wanting to say; the whisperings of hope and His love towards you.

Here is an amazing verse about prayer, and the peace of God that goes beyond all understanding that guards us:

Do not be anxious about anything, but in everything

by prayer and supplication with thanksgiving let

your requests be made known to God. And the

peace of God, which surpasses all understanding,

will guard your hearts and your minds in

Christ Jesus.

Philippians 4: 6-7 ESV

Be encouraged to play praise and worship music in your environment, by tuning into your local Christian radio station or your own playlist, to help set an atmosphere of peace where God is welcome. Like the verse mentioned in a previous chapter: *'Be still and know that I am God.'*

What a great verse to think on in these times. Spending more time with God is so precious, just being calm and at peace with Him, and not being focused on distractions.

Before the virus appeared, it seemed to me that the world was getting busier and busier, but then was suddenly on pause during lockdowns.

Now we are bouncing in and out of isolation periods, normal life isn't what it used to be, and a wanting to return to normality seems to be on pause. But God is not on pause. And if what we knew was 'normal' isn't coming back, don't worry, Jesus is. What a great truth this is to think on with eager expectation; that Jesus will return.

Finally, brethren, whatsoever things are **true**, whatsoever things are **honest**, whatsoever things are **just**, whatsoever things are **pure**, whatsoever things are **lovely**, whatsoever things are of good **report**; if there be any **virtue**, and if there

be any **praise**, think on these things.

Those things, which ye have both learned, and

received, and heard, and seen in me, do: and

the God of **peace** shall be with you.

Philippians 4: 8-9 KJV

With a lot more time at home, many people may be thinking about or getting around to those 'to-do' lists, but if there's a 'to-think-about' list that you've been wanting to get to, then now might be a good time too.

Without the usual rush of life, we can more easily come to God to spend time with Him.

The Lord is my shepherd; I shall not want.

He makes me lie down in green pastures.

He leads me beside still waters.

He restores my soul.

He leads me in paths of

righteousness for his name's sake.

Even though I walk through the

valley of the shadow of death,

I will fear no evil,

for you are with me;

your rod and your staff,

they comfort me.

You prepare a table before me

in the presence of my enemies;

you anoint my head with oil;

my cup overflows.

Surely goodness and mercy shall

follow me all the days of my life,

and I shall dwell in the house

of the Lord forever

Psalm 23 ESV

Here's an incredible verse mentioned in a previous chapter, but in another translation. It is so wonderful that I decided to note it again to encourage you about staying in God's peace as He looks after you:

The Lord will fight for you, and you

shall hold your peace *and* remain at rest.

Exodus 14: 14 AMPC

What does peace look like to you?

_____

_____

_____

_____

_____

_____

_____

_____

_____

_____

_____

_____

_____

_____

_____

_____

_____

_____

_____

_____

_____

_____

_____

PEACE

What does peace feel like?

_____

_____

_____

_____

_____

_____

_____

_____

_____

_____

_____

_____

_____

_____

_____

_____

_____

_____

_____

_____

_____

_____

The Bible says in Philippians 4: 6-7 that God's peace surpasses all understanding. What do you think is meant by this?

_____

_____

_____

_____

_____

_____

_____

_____

_____

_____

_____

_____

_____

_____

_____

_____

_____

_____

_____

_____

Journal your thoughts, prayers and verses about the **peace** of God:

_____

_____

_____

_____

_____

_____

_____

_____

_____

_____

_____

_____

_____

_____

_____

_____

_____

_____

_____

_____

_____

Help

Where does our help come from? Let's see...

If you're feeling helpless, don't give up! Grasp onto our very present help – our ultimate Helper, the Holy Spirit, who is right there with you.

> I lift up my eyes to the hills.
> From where does my help come?
> *My help comes from the LORD,*
> *who made heaven and earth.*
>
> He will not let your foot be moved;
> he who keeps you will not slumber.
> Behold, he who keeps Israel
> will neither slumber nor sleep.
>
> The LORD is your keeper;

the LORD is your shade on your right hand.

The sun shall not strike you by day,

nor the moon by night.

The LORD will keep you from all evil;

he will keep your life.

The LORD will keep

your going out and your coming in

from this time forth and forevermore.

Psalm 121 ESV

Let's lift up our eyes! And look at Jesus!

'Looking up' has been something that has been coming to mind a lot. Recently I lost my favourite writing pen. It usually sits on my desk in the same spot, reserved for special occasions and because it looks pretty there. So when I couldn't find it after much searching I became distressed.

Eventually I even gave up looking for it, and couldn't think of where it could be. But then one day, as I was catching up with a friend on the phone, I happened to notice something as I walked past the tall wall unit. I looked up to see my special pen, right there on top of the wall unit!

As I gratefully retrieved it, the Lord reminded me

of these words 'look up' again. I'd walked past that wall unit a thousand times, but if only I'd looked up, I would have seen it there.

Today, if you're feeling discouraged by your circumstances, I pray for your heart to find comfort in looking up towards Jesus. I pray for a heavenly perspective to open your eyes to the wonderful love of God and His thoughts upon you afresh.

> For we do not have a High Priest who cannot sympathize with our weaknesses, but was in all *points* tempted as *we are, yet* without sin. **Let us therefore come boldly to the throne of grace**, that we may obtain mercy and find grace to help in time of need.
>
> Hebrews 4:15-16 NKJV

This is an amazing verse talking about finding grace to help in our time of need.

Dear friend, is there something you need help with? Be it big or small, firstly know how much God cares for you, and He also cares about what you do. There's nothing too small or too big that

God can't help with. There's nothing impossible for God, and He is outside of time.

I love hearing stories about random acts of kindness. I think it's the unexpected in these situations that interests me, alongside kindness. Kindness is incredibly light-giving and helping someone with something that might seem small to you, might actually be very big to someone else. You never know what others are really going through, and so the act of helping in itself can speak volumes about God's love and light in the midst of darkness.

Being kind or helping someone in need might just be the very thing that gives them hope to keep going, to lift them out of deep despair.

Be kind to yourself also during this time. It's not a normal season to have to endure something that's ongoing in the world like this for so long, so stress levels, anxiety, and depression can creep in more easily. But, God is right there with you, and He knows the importance of you being with other Christians to encourage you too.

If you're struggling, reach out to a friend or family member to talk and pray with.

Having right companionship is vital to counter the effects from all the periods of isolation. Friendship with trusted, likeminded Christians can help cheer you up and remind you of the good that's still in the world.

When I moved to a new city, I missed my friends very much. When we'd catch up on the phone, I'd always feel so much better. Even if nothing was wrong, and we were simply just catching up and talking about God, afterwards it felt like having a hug I didn't know I needed.

God is truly our helper in times of need, and He will help and provide for you, sometimes before you even know you need it too.

I know personally, when myself and my family have received help and kindness in the past, it has encouraged my faith in God. Not only experiencing God as a provider, but also to know and see that He is listening to us, knows our needs, hears our prayers and very much cares.

By the word of Your lips, I have kept away

from the paths of the destroyer.

Uphold my steps in Your paths,

That my footsteps may not slip.

I have called upon You, for You will

hear me, O God;

Incline Your ear to me, *and* hear
my speech.
Show Your marvelous lovingkindness
by Your right hand,
O You who save those who trust *in You*
From those who rise up *against them.*
Psalm 17: 4b – 7 NKJV

Offer the sacrifices of righteousness,
And put your trust in the Lord.
There are many who say,
"Who will show us *any* good?"
Lord, lift up the light of Your
countenance upon us.
You have put gladness in my heart,
More than in the season that their grain
and wine increased.
I will both lie down in peace, and sleep;
For You alone, O Lord, make me dwell
in safety.
Psalm 4: 5 – 8 NKJV

The person who tells of Him in front of men

and says that Jesus is the Son of God, God is

living in that one and that one is living by

the help of God. We have come to know and

believe the love God has for us. **God is love.**

If you live in love, you live by the help of God

and God lives in you.

1 John 4: 15-16 NLV

There are many ways that we might need help during a pandemic. If you've lost a job, you might be praying for financial aid. If you're feeling anxious, your prayer might be for peace. If you're struggling with feeling overwhelmed by the longevity of the pandemic, you might be praying for God's comfort and strength. If you've lost a loved one, your prayers might be full of grief. If you are recovering from the virus, your prayer might be for health and healing.

Whatever your need is today, I pray that you'll receive a deep revelation of who God is as a provider. I pray that every need will be fulfilled, overflowing and more than you need for yourself and to help others also. And I pray for peace and assurance in your heart that God will help you, no matter what it is that you're going through. Our God is mighty to save!

Let's look at these encouraging verses about God's help as a Provider:

The king is not saved by his great army;
a warrior is not delivered by his
great strength.
The war horse is a false hope for salvation,
and by its great might it cannot rescue.
Behold, the eye of the LORD is on those who
fear him,
on those who **hope** in his steadfast love,
that he may deliver their soul from death
and keep them alive in famine.
Our soul waits for the LORD;
he is our help and our shield.
For our heart is glad in him,
because we trust in his holy name.
Let your steadfast love, O LORD, be upon
us, even as we **hope** in you.
Psalm 33: 16-22 ESV

And this same God who takes care of me will supply all your needs from his glorious riches, which have been given to us in Christ Jesus. Now all glory to God our Father forever and ever! Amen.

Philippians 4:19-20 NLT

"That is why I tell you not to worry about everyday life—whether you have enough food and drink, or enough clothes to wear. Isn't life more than food, and your body more than clothing? Look at the birds. They don't plant or harvest or store food in barns, for your heavenly Father feeds them. And aren't you far more valuable to him than they are? Can all your worries add a single moment to your life? "And why worry about your clothing? Look at the lilies of the field and how they grow. They don't work or make their clothing, yet Solomon in all his glory was not dressed as beautifully as they are. And if God cares so wonderfully for wildflowers that are here today and thrown into the fire tomorrow, he will certainly care for you.

Matthew 6: 25 – 30a NLT

As I think about provisions, I'm reminded of the story in the Bible about a widow who had a great need after her husband died (2 Kings 4: 1-7). But the way God provided wasn't for just a small amount – it was more than she needed.

Elisha the prophet, asked her to get jars ready to fill with oil. And not just a few but as many as she could find, from neighbours too. She only had a small jar of olive oil that became many jars of oil that keep pouring out until there were no more jars to fill. Incredible!

In 1 Kings 17:7-16 is another account of a widow who provided for Elijah the prophet during a drought, even though she only had enough food left for one last meal for her son and herself. God provided amazingly and miraculously by ensuring that the jar of flour and the jug of oil she had never ran out until the rain came.

God can supernaturally provide in the most unexpected, amazing ways. In Matthew chapter 17 verses 24-27, it talks about Jesus providing for a temple tax payment by way of a miracle. Jesus told Peter to go fishing and in the first fish he pulled up would be a large coin.

Imagine Peter's curiosity as he did so, and then looked inside the first fish he caught. Sure enough, there it was!

There is something about this example of God's provision that has always stuck with me. I think it's the element of surprise in the unexpected that shows how amazing God is. It has opened my way of thinking to look for the unexpected, surprising ways, as God is not limited, and I know He delights in His children receiving all the things they need.

In Ephesians 3: 20 there's a wonderful verse about God providing more and above what we can ask or think. *God is able to do much more than we ask or think through His power working in us.* (NLV) and I've found this to be true so many times.

The Lord often shows this truth to me through cooking. Sometimes when I'm preparing dinner, I sometimes think that we might not have enough. But after we have finished our meals there's always enough and most often leftovers.

Just like cooking pasta, you start out with an amount that swells up as it's cooked to become much more in quantity than when you first started cooking!

This is a great example of the how the Lord doesn't provide half-heartedly, or provide 'just' enough. But He is the God of more than enough for you and your family in any type of need.

Faith Over Fear

For the LORD your God is living among you.
He is a mighty savior.
He will take delight in you with gladness.
With his love, he will calm all your fears.

Zephaniah 3: 17 a-d NLT

God is our refuge and strength,

always ready to help in times of trouble.

So we will not fear when earthquakes come

and the mountains crumble into the sea.

Let the oceans roar and foam.

Let the mountains tremble as the

waters surge!

A river brings joy to the city of our God,

the sacred home of the Most High.

God dwells in that city; it cannot be destroyed.

From the very break of day, God will protect it.

The nations are in chaos,

and their kingdoms crumble!

God's voice thunders, and the earth melts!

The LORD of Heaven's Armies is here among

us; the God of Israel is our fortress.

Psalm 46: 1 – 7 NLT

HELP

Sometimes we need help with direction. God's Word has some encouraging verses in Isaiah 58:11 about guiding us, meeting our needs and being healthy:

> The LORD will always guide you
> and provide good things to eat
> when you are in the desert.
> He will make you healthy.
> You will be like a garden
> that has plenty of water
> or like a stream that
> never runs dry. (CEV)

In another translation in the NLV, it says the Lord will meet the needs of your soul. Not only does God meet our needs, but also gives us promise of us being like a well of water that never runs dry:

> The Lord will always lead you. He will meet
> the needs of your soul in the dry times and
> give strength to your body. You will be like a
> garden that has enough water, like a
> well of water that never dries up.

God cares about every area of your life, and wants to meet your every need to help you!

> Keep your lives free from the love of money.
> Be happy with what you have. God has
> said, "I will never leave you or let you
> be alone." So we can say for sure,
> *"The Lord is my Helper.* I am not
> afraid of anything man can do to me."
>
> Hebrews 13: 5-6 NLV

When Jesus was on earth, talking to His disciples, He promised them that they wouldn't be alone after He went to heaven. Jesus shared with them about The Holy Spirit coming to earth so we wouldn't be left alone. In some translations it says 'Helper', and in others it says 'Comforter'.

> Jesus said to his disciples: If you love me,
> you will do as I command. Then I will ask
> the Father to send you the Holy Spirit
> who will help you and always be with you.
> **The Spirit will show you what is true.**
>
> John 14: 15-17a CEV

HELP

"If you love Me, you will keep My
commandments. I will ask the Father,
and He will give you another **Helper so
He may be with you forever**— the Spirit of
truth, whom the world cannot receive,
because it does not behold Him or know Him.
You know Him, because **He abides** with you
and will be in you. I will not abandon you as
orphans; I will come to you." (verses 15-18 TLV)

"And I will pray the Father, and he shall give

you another Comforter, that he may abide with

you for ever" (verse 16 KJV)

In this pandemic we are surely in need of comfort,
and we can come to the precious Holy Spirit who
is with us to lean on for comfort. Like leaning on
the shoulder of a friend who's with us.

You may have noticed a few doves featured in this
book's design. After Jesus arose from His water
baptism, the Holy Spirit alighted upon Him in the
form of a dove, and has since been seen as a
symbol of the Holy Spirit. It's a wonderful

reminder that the Holy Spirit is indeed with us during this pandemic.

Jesus, when he was baptized, went up straightway out of the water: and, lo, the heavens were opened unto him, and he saw the Spirit of God descending like a dove, and lighting upon him.

Matthew 3: 16 KJV

Further along in John 14: 25-27, Jesus speaks again about the Father sending the Holy Spirit. This verse then ties in amazingly with the verses about God's peace mentioned in other chapters.

"These things I have spoken to you while being present with you. But the **Helper**, the Holy Spirit, whom the Father will send in My name, He will teach you all things, and bring to your remembrance all things that I said to you. Peace I leave with you, **My peace** I give to you; not as the world gives do I give to you. **Let not your heart be troubled, neither let it be afraid**." (NKJV)

HELP

Let's look at God as a Helper in these reflection questions. What verse stands out to you the most in this chapter?

_____

_____

_____

_____

_____

_____

_____

_____

_____

_____

_____

_____

_____

_____

_____

_____

_____

_____

_____

_____

Faith Over Fear

Journal about a time where someone helped you:

_____

_____

_____

_____

_____

_____

_____

_____

_____

_____

_____

_____

_____

_____

_____

_____

_____

_____

_____

_____

_____

_____

How did it feel at the time?

_____

_____

_____

_____

_____

_____

_____

_____

_____

_____

_____

_____

_____

_____

_____

_____

_____

_____

_____

_____

_____

_____

Faith Over Fear

Write about a time where you have helped someone else?

_____

_____

_____

_____

_____

_____

_____

_____

_____

_____

_____

_____

_____

_____

_____

_____

_____

_____

_____

_____

_____

How did it make you feel?

_____

_____

_____

_____

_____

_____

_____

_____

_____

_____

_____

_____

_____

_____

_____

_____

_____

_____

_____

_____

_____

Faith Over Fear

Write about a time when you knew that help had come from the Lord:

_____

_____

_____

_____

_____

_____

_____

_____

_____

_____

_____

_____

_____

_____

_____

_____

_____

_____

_____

_____

_____

_____

How did you feel before and after:

_____

_____

_____

_____

_____

_____

_____

_____

_____

_____

_____

_____

_____

_____

_____

_____

_____

_____

_____

_____

_____

Note down any other thoughts, prayers and verses about God as our **helper**:

_____

_____

_____

_____

_____

_____

_____

_____

_____

_____

_____

_____

_____

_____

_____

_____

_____

_____

_____

HELP

_____

_____

_____

_____

_____

_____

_____

_____

_____

_____

_____

_____

_____

_____

_____

_____

_____

_____

_____

_____

_____

_____

Worship

In the previous chapter is the wonderful Psalm 46, which was written as a song. In a couple of Bible translations it even has a subheading indicating that it should be sung in soprano – high pitched and bold.

Psalm 46 NLT:

For the choir director: A song of the descendants of Korah,

to be sung by soprano voices.

1 God is our refuge and strength,

always ready to help in times of trouble.

When it mentions nations in chaos in this psalm, it sounds like the writer could've been in a similar situation to us, and yet this was a psalm written to be sung.

Like how God instructed singers to go ahead of the soldiers to worship on the battlefield in 2 Chronicles 20. When Jehoshaphat had heard that there was an army coming against him in Judah, he sought the Lord.

Then God assured him that they wouldn't have to fight, but to stand before the army, and to send out their best singers to sing to the Lord and praise Him.

The victory was theirs when the Lord turned the army of their enemies against themselves!

I recommend reading Jehoshaphat's prayer in chapter 20 and also the rest of this story, where he declared who God is, and I thought he was courageous.

It's quite amazing to read about how God defeated their enemies for them this way. *They just needed to take a stand and worship!*

Let's sing and declare God's truths boldly in the face of any challenges!

Here's a wonderful psalm about thanking and praising God:

Enter his gates with thanksgiving;

go into his courts with praise.

Give thanks to him and praise his name.

For the LORD is good.

His unfailing love continues forever,

and his faithfulness continues to each

generation.

Psalm 100: 4-5 NLT

Another translation says His mercy is everlasting:

Enter into His gates with thanksgiving,

and into His courts with praise! Be thankful

unto Him, and bless His name!

For the LORD is good, His mercy is

everlasting; and His truth endureth

to all generations.

Psalm 100: 4-5 KJ21

Worshipping God during a dark time is a very powerful thing to do.

Be encouraged to spend time in worship and let

all the chaos fade away from the atmosphere as you enter into God's peace that He promises in His Word – a peace that goes beyond understanding.

Worship is very powerful and stops the works of the enemy.

At times, when it's felt like I was experiencing spiritual warfare, I've began worshipping God and playing praise and worship songs. Then suddenly the dark atmosphere lifts. Darkness flees at the sight and sound of light and truth in worship.

Like after days of stormy weather, when the sun breaks through, everything changes. The more the dark storm clouds disappear, and the stronger the sun begins to shine, it's like a welcome, happy sigh of relief. It brings warmth, light, clarity, a calmness, a chance to rest...and I find this is like being in the presence of God.

There's also tremendous power that comes to bring breakthrough when we're worshipping the Most Holy God.

"God is Spirit. Those who worship Him

must worship Him in spirit and in truth."

John 4: 24 NLV

When we enter into God's presence, it's like nothing else matters. Like we've entered into a whole other heavenly realm. It's an opportunity to thank God and bring praise before Him.

In this place, you can rest assured knowing Someone much bigger is in control, honouring Him as a Holy God.

You can step into deep rest, freedom and joy in God's presence as you worship, and let Him wash you with waves of hope, peace and grace, letting your heart be built up with faith and courage.

As some restrictions lifting have meant that some churches have been able to gather again, I've loved hearing about how people have really appreciated worshipping together. There's something special about gathering together.

If you're isolating, don't worry. Be encouraged to spend time worshipping where you are, and reach out to friends and loved ones for vital connection.

Faith Over Fear

Oh come, let us sing to the Lord!
Let us shout joyfully to the **Rock** of
Our salvation.
Let us come before His presence
with thanksgiving;
Let us shout joyfully to Him with
psalms. For the Lord *is* the **great God**,
And the great King above all gods.
In His hand *are* the deep places of
the earth; The heights of the hills
are His also.
The sea *is* His, for He made it;
And His hands formed the dry *land*.
Oh come, let us **worship** and bow down;
Let us kneel before the Lord **our Maker**.
For He *is* our God,
And we *are* the people of His pasture,
And the sheep of His hand.
Psalm 95: 1-7 NKJV

WORSHIP

Write out the lyrics to your current favourite worship song and today's date:

_____

_____

_____

_____

_____

_____

_____

_____

_____

_____

_____

_____

_____

_____

_____

_____

_____

_____

_____

_____

_____

_____

_____

_____

_____

Faith Over Fear

Write out a memory of something powerful that happened, or a revelation you received during worship:

_____

_____

_____

_____

_____

_____

_____

_____

_____

_____

_____

_____

_____

_____

_____

_____

_____

_____

_____

_____

_____

_____

_____

Find and write out a psalm about praising God:

_____

_____

_____

_____

_____

_____

_____

_____

_____

_____

_____

_____

_____

_____

_____

_____

_____

_____

_____

_____

WORSHIP

Journal your own thoughts about what **worship** means to you:

_____

_____

_____

_____

_____

_____

_____

_____

_____

_____

_____

_____

_____

_____

_____

_____

_____

_____

_____

_____

_____

_____

_____

WORSHIP

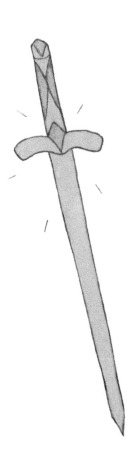

The Day Will Come

As a concluding thought in this last chapter, I'd love to share with you a vision that God had given me earlier, when the pandemic first hit.

It was of a beautiful scene of people with big smiles, looking up into the sunlight that was shining on their faces, standing up as if shaking off the dust of what happened.

As if they were refreshed by the light, and happily embracing a new start.

After seeing this vision, a verse stood out that also compliments this beautifully:

> "The people who sat in darkness
>
> have seen a great light,

Faith Over Fear

And upon those who sat in the

region and shadow of death

Light has dawned."

Matthew 4:16 NKJV

While it may seem like the pandemic is never-ending and so the situations that have come from it, there will come a time when this chaos will cease.

In the meantime, constantly remind yourself of God's goodness and His protection over your life.

Keep strong in faith and prayer, and rest in God's mighty strength to save, and His restorative power.

Light dawns in the darkness

for the upright

Psalm 112: 4a WEB

That day will come. We can wait with a trusting, rested, peace-filled heart knowing we are in God's love and grace, and in Him there is always hope.

THE DAY WILL COME

Write out what a new day looks like for you:

_____

_____

_____

_____

_____

_____

_____

_____

_____

_____

_____

_____

_____

_____

_____

_____

_____

_____

_____

_____

_____

_____

Overall Reflection:

Now we're near the conclusion of this book, write down any thoughts you have about living in faith over fear that has stuck with you:

_____

_____

_____

_____

_____

_____

_____

_____

_____

_____

_____

_____

_____

_____

_____

_____

_____

_____

_____

REFLECTION

What verse or verses has resonated with you the most:

_____

_____

_____

_____

_____

_____

_____

_____

_____

_____

_____

_____

_____

_____

_____

_____

_____

_____

_____

_____

_____

Write out a prayer for what you're going through:

_____

_____

_____

_____

_____

_____

_____

_____

_____

_____

_____

_____

_____

_____

_____

_____

_____

_____

_____

_____

_____

REFLECTION

Underneath each declaration, write the same sentence, changing the words 'you' to 'me', to make a personal declaration over your life. For example: *God keeps me safe.*

God will rescue you

_____

God keeps you safe

_____

God protects you

_____

God cares for you

_____

God provides for you

_____

FAITH SCRIPTURES

Find a verse in your Bible that relates to each sentence topic and write this reference underneath each faith declaration:

God will rescue me

_____

God keeps me safe

_____

God protects me

_____

God cares for me

_____

God provides for me

_____

As a concluding journal entry, write out a praise note to God, if you'd like to, thanking Him for this journaling journey with Him:

_____

_____

_____

_____

_____

_____

_____

_____

_____

_____

_____

_____

_____

_____

_____

_____

_____

_____

_____

_____

Salvation Prayer

If you're reading this book, and are not yet in a relationship with God but feel drawn to His promises in the Bible, then there is something amazing available for you too.

If you openly declare that Jesus is Lord

and believe in your heart that God raised

him from the dead, you will be saved.

Romans 10: 9 NLT

You can say a prayer with me today and become saved, whole, restored and in relationship with a loving God right this very instant:

Dear Jesus

The Bible says that when we confess with our

mouths and believe in our hearts that Jesus is Lord, then we are saved.

I thank you, Jesus, that you died on a cross for me, and by taking all punishment for my sins, I am forgiven, healed, whole and made new again in You.

Thank you, Lord Jesus, that you forgive all my sins – past, present and future.

Thank you for saving my soul – that right now I can become born again in You. I give my heart to you today.

Amen.

If you aren't currently connected to a church, please reach out to a local church near you to connect with fellow believers. There you can find support, encouragement and if you've said the prayer of salvation – please share this good news with them! Many churches are also livestreaming their services online so you can continue to hear words of hope if you're isolating during this time.

Keep being encouraged to choose faith over fear. Be strong, kind and courageous and stay safe in Jesus.

Connection

Dear friend

Well done on going through the journey of journaling with Jesus, delving into faith over fear in your walk with Him.

I hope you have been blessed, found renewed hope, faith and grace in God, and feel encouraged in your relationship with Him. And I hope you are feeling fired up to run the good race of faith, filled with the power of God's Word, to be the light in these dark times!

God bless!

Kataleya, your fellow hope-dweller in Christ

OTHER BOOKS AVAILABLE:

Companion
notebook

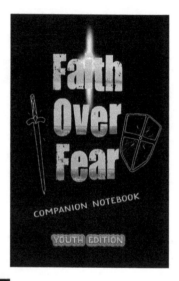

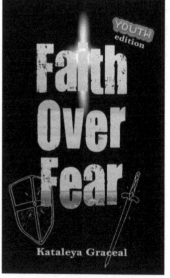

Book

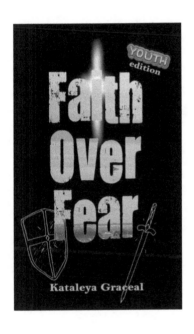

Book and
journal in-one

Lightning Source UK Ltd.
Milton Keynes UK
UKHW020757301222
414627UK00015B/1018